Francesca Grazzi
and
Jack Altman

JPMGUIDES

Contents

This Way Rome

Captivating Capital

Heart of the once mightiest of empires and centre of a universal religion, Rome is almost only incidentally capital of Italy. The great city, so venerated around the world, is regarded with remarkable disdain by the Italians themselves. The haughty, dynamic Milanese consider it woefully provincial, Florentines feel it lacks dignity, others bemoan its cynicism, a carefully nurtured indifference known as *menefreghismo*. Far from protesting, the Romans, often outrageously easygoing, just laugh. They still have the most enchanting capital in Europe.

Rome is fuelled by government, religion and tourism, and it has always been this way. For the city's non-stop flow of pilgrims and tourists, the business of bread and circuses has been variously operated by emperors and senators, popes and cardinals, or presidents and prime ministers. Over the ages, it has produced this citizenry of smiling cynics, all knowing that the only way to make their way through a day in the city is through some variation on the *combinazione*. To get things done, from a place to park the car to an audience at the Vatican or a good seat for the A.S.

Roma or Lazio football match, everybody has to know someone somewhere. Even the city's thousands of clergymen and women seem to participate in this supremely Roman art of clever manoeuvring. Witness the skill with which nuns weave their way through the traffic on motor scooters, or the unnerving sight of priests in mirror-lens sunglasses, like celebrities in the grand old Dolce Vita days on the Via Veneto.

Romans can smile because history is on their side. And it is still everywhere you look, despite centuries of wars and devastating city planning, from despotic popes via 19th-century nationalism to modern fascist dictatorship.

Unabashedly Eternal, the city proclaims its attachment to all the great periods of western civilization. Sipping your cappuccino on the Piazza Navona, you may spot a white-clad policeman trying to stop a Ferrari cruising around Bernini's 17th-century fountain on the site of Emperor Domitian's ancient Roman sports stadium. Pillars, arches and carved masonry of pagan temples have been recycled to build baroque churches among the ruins of the Forum. The modern highways leading north, south, east and west out of the city still bear their ancient names—Via Aurelia, Via Appia, Via Flaminia, Via Cassia.

St Peter's basilica is built over the tomb of the Apostle martyred here in the 1st century. The Vatican palace and museums combine the glories of Etruscan, Greek and Roman antiquities with the treasures of Renaissance and baroque art—as well as a Salvador Dali *Crucifixion* and episcopal robes designed by Matisse. Nowhere is the unity of the ages more eloquently expressed than in the spectacle of a Verdi opera at the monumental Baths of Caracalla.

HISTORY AND MYSTERY

Two modern authors have chosen Ancient Rome as the setting for entertaining whodunnits. American writer Steven Saylor's private investigator Gordianus the Finder gets embroiled in all kinds of racy adventures in *Roman Blood, Arms of Nemesis*, and so on (novels and short stories). Marcus Didius Falco, the lovable sleuth dreamed up by prolific British writer Lindsey Davis, spends most of his time getting into and out of trouble in Rome and various parts of the Roman Empire in *The Silver Pigs* (set largely in Britain), *Shadows in Bronze, Venus in Copper, Time to Depart*, and more. Essential reading for your trip.

Rome's special relationship with eternity inspired painters, sculptors and architects to produce their greatest works of genius here: Michelangelo's Moses and his frescoes for the Sistine Chapel, Bernini's piazza and baldacchino for St Peter's, Caravaggio's formidable paintings for the churches of San Luigi dei Francesi and Santa Maria del Popolo.

A Place For All Ages

Luckily, not everything in Rome is eternal. The town is also attached with equal enthusiasm to the most ephemeral but no less dazzling tastes of modern fashion. Leading away from the famous Spanish Steps—Piazza di Spagna—the narrow streets of Via Condotti and Via Borgognona boast some of the most opulent boutiques in the world. More popular "street fashion" is to be found on nearby and noisier Via Tritone and Via del Corso. Lovers of modern art and antiques head for Via Margutta and Via del Babuino.

The Spanish Steps area is a microcosm of Rome's appeal to all ages. The young crowd hangs out on the steps themselves, elderly aunts congregate at Babington's genteel tea rooms and sophisticated lovers arrange a rendezvous in the more discreet corners of the elegant old Caffé Greco.

The City of Nine Hills

The site chosen for Rome was ideal: relatively sheltered on the coastal plain, centrally situated on a peninsula, with easy access to the sea via the Tiber river for conquest of the Mediterranean. For the magic of numbers, the city has always claimed to be built on seven hills. Building, rebuilding, landfill and earthquakes have reshaped and flattened out the hillocks that in any case never rose higher than 50 m (164 ft) above sea level. On the east bank of the Tiber, crowned by Michelangelo's Piazza Campidoglio, the Capitoline hill is the site of the ancient Roman Capitol—and today's city hall. Immediately to the south, above the Forum, is the Palatine hill where legend says the city was founded on the precise date of April 21, 753 BC.

North of the Capitoline is the Quirinal, which lends its name to the Italian president's palace, while the neighbouring Viminal hill has completely disappeared. On the Esquiline to the east, now more plateau than hill, stands the church of Santa Maria Maggiore, while the park of Celimontana is the main feature of the Celian hill.

On the southern outskirts of the old city, away from the bustle of traffic, is the Aventine, a revered sanctuary in ancient times and now a serene and pleasant residential district.

Across the river, two other hills raise the number to nine—the Janiculum, with its fine park, and finally the state within the city, the Vatican, where a thousand people live and work.

St Peter's basilica and the banks of the Tiber, far from the city bustle.

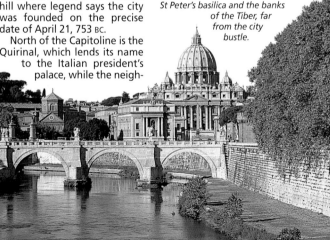

Monarchy to Republic

Legends often have at least one foot in real history. One such is the famous story of Rome being founded on the Palatine Hill in 753 BC by the twin sons of Mars, Romulus and Remus, who were suckled by a she-wolf. Archaeologists seem to agree that the mid-8th century BC is a very likely date for the emergence of the first identifiable Roman township. This would have been a consolidation of several settlements built up on the Palatine, Capitoline and Aventine hills to escape the malarial swamps down by the Tiber. The east bank at the river bend of the modern city centre had been settled with Bronze Age cabins since around 1500 BC.

The twins may also be taken as a dual metaphor for the Italic shepherds and farmers (Romulus) and the more sophisticated Etruscan merchants and craftsmen (Remus). Romulus later killed his brother, just as the Italic tribes of Latins and Sabines absorbed, dominated and ultimately eliminated the Etruscan civilization. It was Etruscan kings who, from the 7th century BC, built the city walls, the Cloaca Maxima sewers to drain the marshlands and the Circus Maximus to entertain the people.

In 509 BC, the Romans overthrew the last of their Etruscan monarchs, Tarquinius Superbus, and established an aristocratic Republic. Over the next 400 years, the governing patricians were constantly at loggerheads with a litigious class of plebeians. The latter elected tribunes to represent them in courts of law in order to settle land disputes, and also to guarantee a regular supply of grain for their daily bread. More disturbingly, the few wealthy plebeians sought social and political equality.

Glories and Horrors of Empire

Apart from the temporary setback of an invasion by the Gauls in 390 BC, Rome progressively overwhelmed the entire Italian peninsula and began to conquer its Mediterranean neighbours. The aristocratic class held on to the spoils of victory and assassinated any recalcitrant champions of the people, such as the Gracchus brothers (in 134 and 123 BC). From civil war emerged another conquering hero, Julius Caesar. His popular dictatorship threatened to upset the delicate balance of patrician power until 44 BC, when he, too, was assassinated.

For the next 17 years, his adopted son had to fight off his rivals Brutus and Mark Antony to claim the title of Rome's first emperor. Augustus Caesar laid the foundations of Rome as the imperial capital of which we can now see the monumental remains—the Forum, temples, senate house, public baths and theatres.

After the crucifixion of Jesus, Jewish and Christian refugees and slaves were deported to Rome. In AD 64, Nero accused Christian revolutionaries of setting fire to the city and had apostles Peter and Paul executed. More constructively, but no less bloodthirstily, Emperor Vespasian had the Colosseum built for gladiator contests. Titus erected a triumphal arch to celebrate his destruction of Jerusalem, while Trajan commemorated victories in the Balkans with a column. Hadrian, the most creative of all the emperor-builders, contributed the magnificent Pantheon, as well as his family mausoleum, today known as the Castel Sant' Angelo. After a chequered history, it has been reconverted into the National Museum.

If Augustus set the tone of the empire's first century as the great age of building, the second was distinguished by philosopher Marcus Aurelius as an era of enlightenment. He improved living conditions for the poor, eased the cruelty of penal law and clamped down on the vicious brutality of gladiators. But Christians, an ever-growing threat to his empire, continued to be persecuted.

Decline began in the 3rd century, when military commanders waged constant power struggles in outposts of northern Europe and Asia. A succession of coups d'état brought no less than 25 emperors within 75 years.

Christians and Barbarians

Emperor Constantine (306–337) saw the apparently inexorable growth of Christianity as a useful means of strengthening his beleaguered hold on the empire. He espoused their cause (though converting only on his deathbed) and moved his capital in 330 to Byzantium, subsequently called Constantinople. Before the resultant split into eastern and western empires, Rome's own Christian foundation was ensured with the building of a host of churches, notably San Giovanni in Laterano and St Peter's basilica.

As the new Byzantine capital prospered, Rome plunged into a dark age of destruction and pillage. Barbarian invasions of Goths and Visigoths, Vandals and Ostrogoths swept through the city from 410. The population had dwindled from a high point of more than a million under Marcus Aurelius to a mere 50,000 by the time the Germanic conqueror, Odoacer, arrived in 476. He deposed the city's last emperor, Romulus Augustulus, so named because he was a mere boy when put on the throne by his father.

Quick work by Pope Leo I a few years earlier put the church on a sounder footing than the city itself. He talked the Huns into bypassing Rome and the Vandals out of putting the entire populace to the sword. On Christmas Day, 800, Charlemagne reinforced the pope's position by having himself crowned emperor in St Peter's.

More violence was to follow. When it was not civil war among local aristocrats, it was foreign attacks—the Arabs in 846, Normans in 1084—and a whole string of papal and imperial armies from inside and outside Italy, until the pope fled to Avignon in 1309. Blood continued to flow in pitched battles between the aristocrats and the populist republicans of tribune Cola di Rienzo.

Renaissance and Church Militant

After Gregory XI decided to end the "Babylonian captivity" and return to Rome in 1376, papal leadership was restored in the city with a new vigour. During the 15th and 16th centuries, despite suspicious murmurs of libertarian individualism, successive popes encouraged the flowering of the Renaissance in the sciences and above all in the arts. St Peter's basilica was completely rebuilt, and every pope added splendid apartments to the Vatican palace. The Vatican Library was founded by scholarly Nicolas V; Julius II, the dynamic warrior pope, called in Michelangelo to paint the ceiling of the Sistine Chapel; while his Medici successor, Leo X, commissioned Raphael and master builder Bramante. Rome recaptured the grandeur of its ancient imperial days, infused with a new spirit of humanism.

Inevitably, with the opulence came corruption and more violence. The armies of Emperor Charles V sacked the city in 1527. The even greater threat of Martin Luther's Protestant Reformation had to be opposed by a tough movement to reassert the authority of the Catholic church. The counter-attack was led by the newly founded Jesuits, who promoted the forceful style of baroque architecture, exemplified by Bernini, as well as emphatically Christian themes in painting and sculpture. Protestants left the city and fled north to Switzerland. For the first time,

Hannibal Carracci's Assumption of the Virgin *illuminates the altar of the church of Santa Maria del Popolo.*

Rome's Jews were confined to a ghetto. The Inquisition weighed in against heretics, philosopher Giordano Bruno was burned alive and Galileo forced to deny his scientific findings.

Capital of Italy

As the 18th century rolled towards revolution, the conservative Austrian Habsburgs took command in Italy, and the papacy was stripped of all real power. When the armies of the French Revolution marched in to proclaim a Roman Republic in 1798, Rome offered no resistance. Napoleon Bonaparte's conquest brought a new sense of nationhood to Italy and, after his defeat in 1814, Rome was the natural choice for the capital. Backed by Giuseppe Garibaldi's fiery Risorgimento army, national patriot Giuseppe Mazzini declared a new republic in 1848, forcing Pope Pius IX to flee. He returned six months later, under the protection of Napoleon III's French troops. The Italian kingdom was finally established in 1862, but minus papal Rome, until Napoleon III's abdication eight years later enabled national troops to capture the city. The pope was again forced into exile, this time to the Vatican, just across the river from the Quirinal palace. In Rome, united Italy at last had a real capital.

Nationalism

The initial spirit of 19th-century nationalism in Rome was one of idealistic independence. By the time the white marble monument to King Vittorio Emanuele II was inaugurated on Piazza Venezia in 1911, this monstrous symbol of the new Italian nationhood exemplified the climate of aggressive jingoism. Its spirit anticipated Italy's enthusiasm for World War I and the advent of the Fascists. After Benito Mussolini led their March on Rome in 1922, King Vittorio Emanuele III made him prime minister, a post that soon turned into a dictatorship.

Il Duce, as Mussolini liked to be known, embarked on the ruthless destruction of historic neighbourhoods to make way for his bombastic new building programmes. It was only natural for the man who regarded himself as the direct heir of the greatest Roman emperors to build the Mussolini Forum, a sports complex now known as Foro Italico. He was ousted in 1943 and assassinated by Italian partisans two years later.

During the Mussolini era, the Lateran Treaty of 1929 proclaimed Catholicism as the state religion and made the Vatican a sovereign state. Cardinal Eugenio Pacelli, who negotiated the concordat with Nazi Germany, became Pope Pius XII in 1939 and was attacked for his passive attitude to persecution of the Jews and the deportation of 2,000 Roman Jews during the German Occupation in 1943. Rome escaped relatively unscathed from wartime bombing by being declared an open city, liberated in 1944.

Dolce Vita

Post-war Rome epitomized the lighter side of Italy's economic recovery. Federico Fellini celebrated the new frivolity of the early 1960s with his film *La Dolce Vita,* in which he portrayed celebrities and hangers-on in the café society of the Via Veneto. Things darkened in the 1970s with terrorist bombings and kidnappings by Neo-Fascists and the extreme left-wing Red Brigade.

At the dawn of the new millennium, Rome celebrated its Jubilee amid great rejoicing. The monuments were given a facelift and many special events organized for the millions of visitors. But its political soul still appears to be fought over by Mafia money-launderers, media magnates and crusading magistrates. Ordinary Romans remain aloof, mainly preoccupied with finding a place to park the car.

Sightseeing

A living open-air museum, Rome offers so much to see that it's best to plan your sightseeing day in advance. We have divided the city into six manageable segments, while all visits entailing a trip by metro or train are listed under Excursions.

ANCIENT ROME

This chapter explores the classical city, from the cluttered remains of the Forum and Colosseum to the peaceful Appian Way, over whose paving stones Roman legions marched on their way to Brindisi to set sail for the Levant and North Africa.

Capitoline Museums E 4*
Piazza del Campidoglio
Daily (except Mon) 9 a.m.–8 p.m. For late-night opening, enquire at the tourist office.
The splendid panoramic terrace of the Caffè Capitolino opens the same hours as the museums.

The extensive collections of these magnificent museums (the oldest in the world) are shared between the Palazzo Nuovo, which is principally consecrated to sculpture, and the Palazzo dei Conservatori opposite. Here, on the first floor, classical pieces are displayed in the original 16th and 17th century décor. You will see the famous Capitoline She-Wolf from the 5th century BC (the twins were added during the Renaissance), and the charming *Spinario*, of uncertain date, depicting a boy seated on a rock and removing a thorn from his foot.

The picture gallery on the second floor displays canvases by masters such as Caravaggio, Guercino, Pier Francesco Mola, Titian and Veronese. There is also a collection of porcelain.

The courtyard was chosen to display the huge "spare parts"—a head, a foot and a forearm—from a colossal statue of Constantine, as big as a four-storey building, discovered in 1487 in the Basilica of Maxentius in the Roman Forum.

Piazza del Campidoglio E 4
Michelangelo designed this beautiful trapezoidal square on the top of the Capitoline, as well as the Cordonata, the great stairway leading down to Via del Teatro di Marcello. He also drew the plans for the Palazzo Nuovo and was responsible for the renovation of the façades of the Palazzo dei Conservatori and the Palazzo Senatorio (Town Hall).

Roman Forum F 4–5
Foro Romano
Entrances: Largo Romolo e Remo, Piazza Santa Maria Novella 53
Daily 9.30 a.m.–3.30 p.m.

References correspond to the fold-out map at the end of the guide.

Before the Forum could be built, the marshland chosen for its site below the Quirinal, Viminal, Palatine and Capitoline hills had to be drained. The Cloaca Maxima (Great Drain), begun by Tarquinius Priscus in about 600 BC, is still in operation! (It empties into the Tiber near the Ponte Palatino.)

The Forum was the market place. Archeological excavations started in the 18th century are still under way. The view of the ensemble from the top of the Campodoglio is magnificent: you can see the Via Sacra which crosses the Forum and was once the route taken by triumphal and religious processions. Among all the temples, columns, basilicas, arches, public baths, rostra and ancient palaces, note the Arch of Titus and the remains of the grandiose Basilica of Maxentius and Constantine, richly decorated in marble and bronze.

Imperial Fora F 4

  : Via dei Fori Imperiali
  : Guided tours Sat, Sun 11 a.m. and 3 p.m. Visits with audioguides: Fora Traiani and Augusto Tues, Sun 10 a.m.–noon; Fori di Cesare and Nervia: Fri, Sat, Sun 10–10.50 a.m. and 3–3.50 p.m.

When the demands of public life outgrew the Roman Forum, the emperors built other Fora, all in the same area. In the centre of the Julian Forum (54–46 BC), there is a temple to Venus Genetrix (Tempio di Venere Genitrice) and the vestiges of the Basilica Argentaria. There followed the Forum Augusti (31–2 BC), then the Forum Vespasiani (AD 69–75). Domitian began yet another Forum which was completed by Nerva in AD 97. The last to be built, and the best-preserved, was the Forum Traiani (AD 107–113), a masterpiece by the architect Apollodorus of Damascus, financed with booty captured from the Dacians (from a region roughly corresponding to today's Romania).

Trajan's Column F 4

  : Colonna Traiana
  : Via dei Fori Imperiali

One of the few ancient monuments which are still almost intact, this column is 40 m (131 ft) high. Decorated with a spiral bas-relief, originally painted in bright colours, it illustrates scenes from the wars against the Dacians. Tiny windows throw a faint light onto an interior spiral staircase which climbs to the very top (closed to the public).

Palatine Hill F 5

  : Access through the Forum
  : Piazza Santa Maria Nova 53
  : Same opening hours as the Forum.

According to legend, this is where Romulus and Remus were suckled by a she-wolf. Covered in pine trees and flowers, it is one of Rome's most attractive archeological sites. The splendid Farnese Gardens (Orti Farnesiani) nearby are open to the public. The emperors built their palaces on the Palatine Hill, from where they governed the 54 million inhabitants of a world stretching from the Atlantic to the Euphrates, from the Sahara to the Danube. There's a lot to see here, notably the emperor's private residence, Domus Augustana, the Domus Flavia and the house of Livia.

Santa Maria in Cosmedin E 5
⋮ Piazza della Bocca della Verità
Founded in the 6th century and rebuilt and restored several times, this beautiful church served the Greek community. Very simple, it houses some magnificent mosaics and other works of art such as the Bishop's Throne and the Gothic baldaquin of the high altar. Under the porch is the **Bocca della Verità**, a thick disc of marble sculpted with a face, probably a well-cover dating from the 4th century BC. Tradition has it that this "Mouth of Truth" would bite the hand of a liar: to test the fidelity of a spouse it was enough to place his or her hand in the mouth.

The square in front of the church contains an ancient circular temple dedicated to Hercules, a rectangular temple dedicated to Portunus, and the 4th-century Arch of Janus.

Santa Sabina E 6
⋮ Piazza Pietro d'Illiria 1
Restoration work undertaken in 1914 returned this early Christian church to its primitive simplicity. Light from 9th-century windows illuminates the white Corinthian columns. The carved 5th-century cedar wood doors have 18 panels illustrating scenes from the Bible.

San Pietro in Vincoli F 4
⋮ Piazza di San Pietro in Vincoli 4A
Under the altar are the chains from Jerusalem and Rome which bound the imprisoned Saint Peter. Legend has it that when the two were put in contact, the links miraculously welded together. The church is chiefly known for the tomb of Julius II, a masterpiece by Michelangelo but nevertheless falling short of the original design which envisaged forty statues. Before beginning to work, Michelangelo spent eight months at Carrara searching for perfect blocks of marble. Only after several years, in 1513, did he succeed in completing three statues, that of Moses and those of Jacob's wives,

Rachel and Leah. Look particularly at the hands of Moses; you can almost see the blood coursing through the veins. He bears horns, the result of a mistranslation in the Vulgate of the Hebrew for "light".

Colosseum F–G5

- Piazza del Colosseo, entrance near Arch of Constantine
- Daily 9.30 a.m. –3.30 p.m.

Emperor Vespasian chose the site of Nero's private lake for the Colosseum, destined for the entertainment of the populace. Its inauguration by Titus in 80 AD was marked by a celebration which lasted for 100 days, during which 5,000 wild beasts were slaughtered. Of elegant design, the building had 80 arcades leading to a system of staircases, the *vomitoria*, which provided the 55,000 spectators with easy access to their seats.

Despite the ravages of time, the Colosseum remains one of the most majestic monuments of Ancient Rome.

Arch of Constantine F 5

- Arco di Costantino
- Piazza del Colosseo

This is the largest and best-preserved of the ancient Roman triumphal arches. It was built by the Senate and people to celebrate the victory of Emperor Constantine over Maxentius in AD 312. The friezes and reliefs were taken from earlier monuments built during the reigns of Domitian, Hadrian, Trajan and Marcus Aurelius.

Case romane F 4

- Santi Giovanni e Paolo
- Entrance on Via Clivio di Scauro
- Guided tours restricted to groups of max. 25 persons; reservation only, tel. 06 70 45 45 44.
- Closed Tues, Wed

On three underground floors beneath the basilica, a maze of ancient dwellings comprising 20 rooms that date back to the 2nd century BC. They were joined in the 3rd century AD to form a large patrician residence, and the basilica was built on top in the 5th century. Many of the rooms are decorated with frescoes, mosaics and marble inlay, all carefully restored.

Domus Aurea G 4

- Via della Domus Aurea
- Daily (except Tues)
- 9 a.m.–7.45 p.m.

Nero's splendid villa, the Golden House, was built in 64 BC, after a great fire had destroyed the city. It used to face a great lake surrounded by vineyards, and the entire façade was gilded. After Nero's death, Vespasian had the

Sightseeing

Stately line-up in the Forum, in front of the temple of Antoninus Pius and Faustina.

lake drained and built the Colosseum in its place. The upper storeys of the villa were razed to make way for Trajan's Baths. The remaining rooms, below ground level, were discovered during the Renaissance. Some of the grand frescoed halls, painted to resemble grottoes, are thought to have inspired the "grotesque" style used by Raphael and his contemporaries. Part of the decoration of the vaulted nymphaeum is intact.

Parco del Celio G 6
South of the Colosseum, this is one of Rome's most beautiful green spaces. Quiet and well-maintained, it is the ideal location for relaxation.

San Clemente G 5
Via San Giovanni in Laterano
Daily 9 a.m.–12.30 p.m. and 3–6 p.m. Sun and holidays 10 a.m.–12.30 p.m. and 3–6 p.m.
Underground rooms: 9 a.m.–12.30 p.m. and 3–6 p.m.
The basilica is made up of three superimposed buildings. In the upper church (12th-century) note the handsome marble paving, and the glittering mosaic in the apse

representing the Triumph of the Cross. From the sacristy, stairs descend to the 4th century basilica adorned with faded Roman frescoes. From the nave, ancient steps lead to a network of passages and rooms which were probably Roman houses, and a pagan temple dedicated to the cult of Mithras.

San Giovanni in Laterano H 6

Piazza San Giovanni in Laterano
Fifteen statues of Christ and various saints crown the 18th-century façade of St John Lateran, the Cathedral of Rome, built between 313 and 318 on even more ancient foundations. Until 1870, the Popes were crowned here. Today, the Pope celebrates Mass in the cathedral on Maundy Thursday. The baptistry dates from the reign of Constantine but was given its present octagonal form in 432. The peaceful cloister, surrounded by small twisting columns encrusted with mosaics, is exquisite.

The Scala Santa, the staircase on the east side of the square, is built of 28 steps which Saint Helen brought from Jerusalem. They are supposed to be from the staircase which Jesus descended when leaving the palace of Pontius Pilate after his condemnation. Penitents climb it on their knees.

Baths of Caracalla G 6

Viale delle Terme di Caracalla
Tues–Sun 9 a.m.–3.30 p.m.;
Mon 9 a.m.–1 p.m.
These baths (completed in AD 217) could hold 1,500 people. The whole treatment took place in several stages. After warming-up exercises, the body was oiled and scraped from head to foot. Then the client entered the laconicum to perspire and afterwards took a hot bath in the *calidarium*. After a short rest to cool down in the tepidarium and then the *frigidarium*, there came a session in the cold-water swimming pool, the *natatio*. The last stage was a perfumed massage—early aromatherapy!

For spiritual renewal there were libraries, art galleries, gardens and terraces serving as a solarium—in fact, everything which a modern leisure-centre now provides.

Aurelian Wall

Mura Aureliane
Vantage point at Porta San Sebastiano
(off map, dir. G6)
Daily (except Mon) 9 a.m.–7 p.m.
Begun by the Emperor Aurelius in 270 AD, these ramparts protected the city from attack by Barbarian tribes. Covering a length of 18 km (11 miles), with 18 gates and 381 towers, the wall encloses most of

the principal historic monuments of the city. San Sebastiano Gate, southeast of the Baths of Caracalla, has an interesting museum devoted to the wall and the Appian Way, and from there you can walk along part of the parapets.

Appian Way
- Via Appia Antica
- (off map, dir. G6)

This major road went all the way to Brindisi. It was lined with splendid monuments, of which there are only a few vestiges remaining today: the church known as **Domine Quo Vadis** (Whither goest thou, Lord?), where Saint Peter is said to have met Jesus while escaping from Rome; the tomb of Cecilia Metella; the mausoleum of Romulus, son of Maxentius; and the catacombs of Saint Calixtus and Saint Sebastian.

Catacombs of St Calixtus
- Catacombe di San Callisto
- Via Appia Antica 110
- (off map, dir. G6)
- Daily (except Wed, Jan and Feb)
- 8.30 a.m.–noon and
- 2.30–5 p.m. (5.30 p.m. in summer)

These catacombs, which are built on four levels, have up to now only been partially explored. Frescoes decorated the most important crypts, such as the Crypt of the

Popes, where at least 14 Pontiffs are buried.

Catacombs of St Sebastian
- Catacombe di San Sebastiano
- Via Appia Antica 136
- (off map, dir. G6)
- Daily (except Sun and Nov 15 to Dec 15) 8.30 a.m.–noon and 2.30–5.30 p.m. in summer;
- to 5 p.m. in winter

The remains of martyred Saint Sebastian were removed from the crypt beneath the basilica in the 9th century. The walls are covered with graffiti, invocations to Saints Peter and Paul, whose remains possibly lay hidden here during one of the periods when Christians were persecuted.

Catacombs of Domitilla
- Catacombe di Domitilla
- Via delle Sette Chiese 283
- (off map, dir. G 6)
- Daily (except Tues and all Jan) 8.30 a.m.–noon and 2.30–5 p.m. (5.30 p.m. in summer)

The burial place of Saint Flavia Domitilla who converted to Christianity in the 1st century, these catacombs were excavated in the 4th century when the Basilica of Saints Nereus and Achilleus was built on the site. On several levels, they are decorated with frescoes of classical and Christian scenes.

HISTORIC CENTRE

The main street in central Rome is the Via del Corso, stretching for a mile from the Piazza del Popolo to the Piazza Venezia. It is lined with shops, palaces and churches, and is particularly lively at the end of the day, when it is thronged with people enjoying their evening stroll. In this chapter we have included the sights on both sides of the Corso, and the historic centre ringed by the Tiber.

Piazza del Popolo E 1

The Porta del Popolo, a triumphal arch pierced in the Aurelian Wall, used to be the entry point for visitors coming from the north: the Latin inscription reads "For a happy and joyful entry, 1655". The arch opens onto Bernini's lovely oval square, renovated by Giuseppe Valadier (1816–24). The obelisk of Ramses II in the centre once adorned the Circus Maximus. The twin churches of Santa Maria dei Miracoli and Santa Maria di Montesanto guard the entry to the Via del Corso.

Santa Maria del Popolo E 1
⠿ Piazza del Popolo 12
The interior of this church "of the people" boasts many important works of art. The chapels belong to Rome's most illustrious families. The Della Rovere Chapel on the right boasts a fresco by Pinturicchio (1454–1513); the Cerasi Chapel to the left of the choir contains two masterpieces by Caravaggio: *The Crucifixion of Saint Peter* and *The Conversion of Saint Paul*. The Chigi Chapel, the best of all, was designed by Raphael.

Via del Babuino E 1
Antique dealers have colonized this street leading from Piazza del Popolo to Piazza di Spagna. A reclining statue of the satyr Silenus, mistaken by early inhabitants for a monkey, gave rise to its name.

Piazza di Spagna E 2
All foreign visitors to Rome are irresistibly attracted to the travertine steps of the Trinità dei Monti church. Perhaps they come to take tea in Babington's Tea Rooms, or a hamburger in the city's first McDonald's. It's the perfect place to stop for a rest, for writing postcards, for people-watching, for taking photos in front of the spring azaleas—or simply for basking in the pleasure of being in Rome… The square is named after the Spanish Embassy which stood here in the 17th century. Bernini's **Fontana della Barcaccia** is the

first fountain he ever built. If you look closely at the prow of the boat you will see three bees, the emblem of Pope Urban VIII.

Ara Pacis Augustae E 2
- Via di Ripetta
- Closed for renovation

The "Altar of Augustan Peace" is an important example of Roman art from the Augustinian period (1st century BC).The Carrara marble altar, protected by glass walls, is decorated with friezes and reliefs depicting the Emperor Augustus and his wife Livia in the company of numerous priests, magistrates, patricians and gods. It commemorates the peace achieved by Augustus after campaigns in Gaul and Spain, and was reconstructed in 1937–38 from bits and pieces discovered beneath the foundations of the Palazzo Fiano.

Piazza di Trevi E 3
- Via delle Muratte/via della Stamperia

The **Fontana di Trevi**, the biggest, most famous, most-photographed fountain (1732–51) in Rome is by Nicola Salvi and represents the ocean. Neptune in the centre is flanked by two Tritons guiding sea horses (the work of Bracci). Filippo della Valle carved the figures in the side niches, Abundance on the left

and Salubrity on the right. Bathing is strictly forbidden, whatever Anita Ekberg did in *La Dolce Vita*. Turn your back to the fountain and throw in a coin—you will be sure to return to Rome.

Galleria Colonna F 3
- Palazzo Colonna
- Via della Pilotta 17
- Sat 9 a.m.–1 p.m. Other days by request on tel. 06 678 43 50.
- Closed in August.

This is the largest private collection in Rome, with magnificent paintings from the 14th to the 18th centuries. You can admire works by Tintoretto, Old Palma, Bronzino, Veronese and Carracci, among others.

Palazzo Venezia E 4
- Via del Plebiscito 118
- Museum open daily (except Mon) 8.30 a.m.–7.30 p.m.)

Cardinal Pietro Barbo, the future Pope Paul II, ordered construction of this palace in 1455. It became the property of the state in 1916. Mussolini used it as his head-quarters and installed his office in the Sala del Mappamondo, named after a fresco showing the world as it was known in 1495. Magnificent collections of early Renaissance paintings, sculptures, tapestries and ceramics.

Column of Marcus Aurelius E 3

Colonna di Marco Aurelio
Piazza Colonna

The column, 30 m (98 ft) high and 3.7 m (12 ft) in diameter, was erected after the death of Marcus Aurelius in 180 AD to commemorate his victories over the barbarians at the Danube frontier. It is built of 28 marble blocks with 20 detailed spiral carvings illustrating his military campaigns. Originally, they would have been painted. An interior staircase winds up to the top, surmounted by a statue of Saint Paul, added in 1589 when the reliefs of the pedestal were removed.

WINDOW SHOPPING

The elegant Roman ladies have a refined taste and are fond of handmade goods. The shopping district fills a triangle with its points at Piazza del Popolo, Piazza Navona and Piazza di Spagna.

The great names in Italian fashion are all to be found in the pedestrian streets between Piazza di Spagna and Via del Corso. The most luxurious of the shops have their premises in medieval or Renaissance palaces.

The great jewellers (gioiellerie) are clustered around Piazza di Spagna, while the goldsmiths' workshops are mostly near the Campo di Fiori.

Leather articles, often handmade by Italian craftsmen, are appreciated the world over. The finest and most expensive shoes are found in and around Via Condotti. For more affordable prices look around the Trevi Fountain area, or visit the markets. And all over the city you'll find a wide choice of gifts and souvenirs, usually exquisitely displayed.

Designer boutiques to look out for:

Via del Babuino: Chanel at No. 98–101 and a branch of Emporio Armani at 140.

Via Bocca di Leone: Valentino (for ladies) at No. 16 (ladies); Gianni Versace (for ladies) at 27; Mariella Burani at 28.

Via Borgognona: Dolce & Gabbana at No. 8, Gianni Versace for men at 25; Laura Biagiotti at 43; and several branches of Fendi.

Via Condotti: Gucci at No. 8; Bulgari at 10; Valentino at 13; Max Mara at 19; Buccellati jewellers at 31, Trussardi at 49; Campanile (expensive shoes) at 58; Furla at 55; Ferragamo's fabulous shops at 64–66 (men) and 73–74 (ladies' clothing and leatherware); Prada at 88.

Via Frattina: Brighenti at No. 7/8 where the stars buy their lingerie; Max Mara at 28, Testa, for smart young men at 105; Fausto Santini (trendy shoes) at 120–121.

Piazza di Spagna: Sergio di Cori at No. 53; Dior at 74, Missoni at 77.

Galleria Doria Pamphilj E 3

Palazzo Doria Pamphilj
Piazza del Collegio Romano 1A
Daily (except Thurs)
10 a.m.–5 p.m.

A priceless private collection of more than 400 paintings dating from the 16th to 18th centuries. Marvellous canvases by Caravaggio, Raphael, Titian, Reni, Velasquez, Vanvitelli.

Palazzo di Montecitorio E 3

Piazza di Montecitorio
Closed to the public.

Built by Pope Innocent X in 1653 according to a design by Bernini, this palace was completed in 1697 by Carlo Fontana and became the Vatican Tribunal. The obelisk of Psammetichus II which stands in front of the façade was part of the spoils brought from Heliopolis by Augustus. The palace has been the meeting place of the Chamber of Deputies since 1871.

Pantheon E 3

Piazza della Rotonda
Mon–Sat 8.30 a.m.–7.30 p.m.;
Sun 9 a.m.–6 p.m.

Hadrian built this temple dedicated to all the gods, which in the Middle Ages became a church. At the centre of the cupola, a unique opening of 9 m (30 ft) lets in the light like an "eye" in the firmament. Among the treasures of the Pantheon are the tombs of several kings of Italy, and the tomb of Raphael.

Piazza della Minerva E 3

In 1630, an elephant was brought to Rome, and it's more than likely that Bernini went to study it closely, because his life-size elephant here supporting an obelisk is perfect in every detail, apart from an over-long trunk.

This monument was erected in 1667 in honour of Pope Alexander VII. The Latin inscription reads: "Whomsoever sees the images inscribed by the Egyptians in their wisdom, the images borne by this elephant, the strongest of all the animals, may he ponder the following: have strength of character and let profound wisdom be your support".

The 6th-century BC red granite obelisk is surmounted by a cross and the Papal arms.

Piazza Navona D 3

Built on the site of the Stadium of Domitian, this square was designed to be filled with water to provide nautical entertainment.

The **Fontana dei Fiumi** (Fountain of the Four Rivers) in the centre is by Bernini (1651). The four great figures each symbolize a river

Domitian's oval-shaped athletics stadium has become one of Rome's most pleasingly harmonious squares, Piazza Navona.

representing, in turn, a continent. Europe is personified by Danube, gesticulating vehemently. Ganges, oar in hand, represents Asia. Nile is hidden under a hood, supposedly to signify the mysterious side of the dark continent. For his depiction of the Americas, in the wild, bearded figure of Rio de la Plata, Bernini seems to have let his imagination run amok: he is staring—some say fearfully—at the nearby church of Sant'Agnese in Agone.

The two other fountains in the square are by Giacomo della Porta and renovated by Bernini, who designed the central figure of the

Fontana del Moro. The obelisk standing in the middle of the square comes from the Circus of Maxentius. Domitian had it carved with hieroglyphs showing Egyptian divinities paying their respects to Roman emperors.

Sant'Agnese in Agone D 3

Piazza Navona

Built between the 8th and 12th centuries on the site of the martyrdom of Saint Agnes, the church took on its present form in 1652, a design by Girolamo and Carlo Rainaldi, modified later by Bernini, Pietro de Cortone and

LAMB TO THE SLAUGHTER

The saint to whom the church Sant'Agnese in Agone, on Piazza Navona, is dedicated, was a 4th-century virgin martyr. The 13-year-old daughter of an aristocratic family was slain for refusing to marry the noble suitor her parents had chosen for her. Her symbol is the lamb and on her feast day, January 21, a pallium vestment made from the wool of a specially blessed lamb is given by the pope to a particularly worthy archbishop. The ritual dates back to the 6th century.

lastly by Francesco Borromini who was responsible for the concave façade, the dome and the campaniles.

San Luigi dei Francesi D 3
: Via Santa Giovanna d'Arco
The French national church, completed around 1589, contains the tombs of many distinguished Frenchmen, including the painter Claude Lorrain, directors of the Académie Française, and soldiers fallen during the Roman Republic in 1848 or during the Italian Campaign of 1944–45. In a chapel on the left is a monument raised by Chateaubriand to the memory of Pauline de Beaumont. In the Contarelli Chapel, there are many fine canvases by Caravaggio: *The Calling of Saint Matthew, The Martyrdom of Saint Matthew,* and *Saint Matthew and the Angel,* his earliest great religious works.

Santa Maria della Pace D 3
: Vicolo dell'Arco della Pace
Work on this church was begun in 1482 at the behest of Pope Sixtus IV to celebrate the end of the war with the Turks. The cloister (1504) is by Bramante. The Chigi Chapel on the right is decorated with frescoes by Raphael depicting the four Sybils. Baldassarre Peruzzi painted the frescoes in the Ponzetti Chapel on the left. A new façade, with circular entrance, was added in the 17th century by Pietro de Cortone.

Palazzo Altemps D 3
: Piazza Sant'Apollinare 44
: Tues–Sun 9 a.m.–7.45 p.m.,
: sometimes later in summer
Construction of this superb palace was begun in 1477 but it was not completed until the end of the 16th century. It housed the collections of antiquities gathered by Cardinal Marcus Psiticus Altemps and his heirs, and a great library which has been transferred to the Vatican. The palace now belongs to the State and is part of the Museo Nazionale Romano. Apart from the Egyptian collection,

and the 16 Altemps sculptures, don't miss the remarkable Ludovisi Boncompagni collection. Great construction works were carried out in Rome during the Counter-Reformation, and whenever statues were excavated, they were put on sale, day by day. Boncompagni snatched up several and had them restored by sculptors such as Bernini—the repair work is clearly indicated.

The entire palace is beautifully decorated with baroque paintings: on the first floor, for example, the Sala delle Prospettive Dipinte is adorned with landscapes and hunting scenes observed through windows painted in trompe-l'œil.

Sant'Ivo alla Sapienza D 3

Corso del Rinascimento 40

There's nothing run-of-the-mill in this church, recognizable from afar by its helicoidal lantern-light surmounted by a cross. Seen close-up, this construction by Borromini (1643–60) is one of the most dynamic achievements of Roman baroque. The ground plan is based on two superimposed triangles with curved sides forming a Star of David. With white-painted walls, the church is light and airy; the four levels of the dome are decorated with stuccco of stars, crowns and hosts of angels.

Palazzo Madama D 3

Corso del Rinascimento
Open the first Sat of the month
10 a.m.–6 p.m.,
upon written request

Built in the 16th century by the Florentine family of bankers, the Medici, this palace took the name of "Madama" Margaret of Austria, the illegitimate daughter of Emperor Charles V, and wife of Alessandro dei Medici. The sumptuous baroque façade dates from the 17th century. Since 1871, the palace is the seat of the Italian Senate.

Sant'Andrea della Valle D 4

Piazza Sant'Andrea della Valle

Puccini set the first act of *Tosca* in a chapel of this church.

It is renowned for its dome, which is the highest in Rome after St Peter's and, like the façade, the work of Carlo Maderno. Several 17th-century artists contributed to its decoration: Borromini for the lantern; Lanfranco for the frescoes of the cupola, the *Vision of Paradise;* Domenico Zampieri for the frescoes of the apse and the pendentives (the triangular spaces between the tops of the columns and the cupola). Inside are fine paintings by Calabrese, Domenichino *(St John the Baptist)* and Mattia Preti *(Crucifixion of St Andrew).*

Museo Barracco D 4

- Corso Vittorio Emanuele II 166a
- Daily 9 a.m.–7 p.m.

The delightful palace which is home to this museum is known as the Piccola Farnesina. The collection was assembled in the 19th century by Senator Barracco and was moved here in the early 20th century. It consists of many remarkable ancient Babylonian, Assyrian, Egyptian, Etruscan, Greek and Roman sculptures.

Galleria Spada D 4

- Palazzo Spada
- Piazza Capo di Ferro 13
- Daily (except Mon)
- 8.30 a.m.–7.30 p.m.

The majestic Spada Palace was built in the 1550s for Cardinal Capo di Ferro and later for the Cardinals Spada, two brothers who confided the project to Bernini and Borromini. The latter was responsible for a trompe-l'œil colonnade in the garden which gives the impression of being four times longer than its actual length of 9 m (30 ft).
Great art-lovers, the two cardinals assembled a magnificent collection of 16th- and 17th-century paintings (including works by Rubens, Dürer, Andrea del Sarto, Titian, Guido Reni and Guercino), classical sculpture and 18th-century furniture.

Palazzo Farnese D 4

- Piazza Farnese
- Visits by request:
- fax 06 686 01 331

Built by Cardinal Alessandro Farnese from 1517, this imposing palace was the inspiration for other princely palaces. Among the architects who worked on it were Sangallo the Younger, Michelangelo and Giacomo della Porta. Today it is the residence of the French ambassador.

Campo dei Fiori D 4

- Piazza Campo dei Fiori
- Mon–Sat 7 a.m.–1.30 p.m.

In the centre of the old city, this is Rome's most famous and most picturesque market. The range of shining fresh fruit, vegetables, cheeses, salami, fish and olives on the stalls is of the highest quality and the displays are as beautiful as still-lifes. The old ghetto is clustered around the campo, and you can look around many goldsmiths' workshops in the area, near the Ponte Sisto and along Via del Pellegrino, Via dei Coronari and Via dell'Orso.

San Carlo ai Catinari E 4

- Piazza B. Cairoli

This church of the order of Barnabites is dedicated to Saint Carlo Borromeo, Archbishop of

Milan. It owes its name to the local makers of wooden basins (catinari). The beautiful façade in travertine marble was completed in 1638. Paintings and frescoes illustrate the life of the Saint, canonized in 1610. The church houses one of Giovanni Lanfranco's finest works, The Annunciation.

Piazza Mattei E 4

All the palaces around the piazza belonged to the Mattei famly. Perhaps the most outstanding is the Mattei de Grove palace with its remarkable collection of old marble in the courtyard. The family ordered the charming **Fontana delle Tartarughe** (Turtle Fountain) to brighten up their square. Made between 1581 and 1584 by Taddeo Landini from a design by Giacomo della Porta, it shows four youths each standing with one foot on a dolphin's head. It remains a mystery as to who was inspired to place four turtles on the edge of the basin a century later.

MARKETS

For local colour, there's nothing to beat rummaging around the city markets. Apart from the famous food market in Campo dei Fiori, there are plenty of others around town.

To the north of the Vatican, along Via Trionfale (B 1), the wholesale flower market, **Mercato dei Fiori**, is open to the public on Tuesdays 10.30 a.m.– 1 p.m. You can buy plants and seeds, as well as flowers, and many exotic species.

In the historic centre, on Largo della Fontanella Borghese (E 2), the **Mercato delle Stampe**, open Saturday and Sunday 9 a.m.–7 p.m., does not deal in stamps but in books and prints.

South of the Termini railway station, **Piazza Vittorio Emanuele II** (H 4) hosts a large food market, with many other stalls, too (clothing, pots and pans, leatherware, toiletries), from Monday to Saturday 7 a.m.–2 p.m.

The flea market is held in Trastevere, at **Porta Portense** (D 6), Sundays only, 6.30 a.m.–2 p.m. It sells everything from kittens to wardrobes. If you feel up to haggling in Italian, you may get a bargain.

South of town (off map dir. E 6, metro line B to Piramide), the **Mercato di Testaccio** is held Monday to Saturday 6 a.m.–1.30 p.m. The covered part is devoted to food; there are a few clothing stalls outside.

At **Via Sannio**, near San Giovanni in Laterano (H 6), along part of the Aurelian Wall, you can buy new and second-hand clothing, and shoes. Open Monday to Friday 8 a.m.–1 p.m.; Saturday 8 a.m.–6 p.m.

Gesù E 4

⋮ Piazza del Gesù

Begun by Vignola in 1568 and finished by Giacomo della Porta in 1584, this was the first Jesuit church in the city, and influenced Roman baroque religious architecture for almost a century. Financed by Cardinal Alessandro Farnese, the church is very sober outside, but in the 17th century the interior was enriched by splendid works of art: the frescoes of the vault by Giovanni Battista Gaulli (Baciccia); the Altar of Saint Ignatius, which incorporates an enormous block of lapis-lazuli; the rooms of Saint Ignatius with an astonishing corridor in trompe-l'œil by Andrea Pozzo.

ROMAN WHO'S WHO

A short list to help you find your way among the galaxy of Italian painters and sculptors whose works you'll see in Rome. The name commonly used in Italy is in bold type, the English version, where applicable, in *italics*.

– Andrea d'Agnolo, known as **Andrea del Sarto**, 1486–1531
– Giovanni Battista Gaulli, known as **il Baciccia** or **Baciccio**, 1639–1709
– Donato di Angelo, known as **Bramante**, 1444–1514
– Gian Lorenzo **Bernini**, 1598–1680
– Francesco Castelli, known as **Borromini**, 1599–1667
– Pietro Cerroni known as **Cavallini**, c.1250– c.1340
– Michelangelo Merisi or Amerighi, known as **Caravaggio**, c.1571–1610
– Annibale **Carracci**, 1560–1609
– Domenico Zampieri, known as **il Dominichino**, 1581–1641
– Guido di Pietro, Fra Giovanni da Fiesole, known as **Il Beato** or **Fra Angelico**, 1387–1455
– Giovanni Francesco Barbieri, known as **il Guercino**, 1591–1666
– **Michelangelo** Buonarroti, 1475–1564
– Jacopo Negretti, known as **Palma il Vecchio** *(Old Palma)*, c.1480–1528. His brother's grandson, also called Jacopo (1544–1628) is known as **Palma il Giovane** *(Palma the Younger)*.
– Francesco Mazzolo, known as **il Parmigianino**, 1503–1540
– Bernardino di Betto, known as **il Pinturicchio** ("the dauber"), 1454–1513
– **Raffaello** Sanzio *(Raphael)*, 1483–1520
– Antonio Cordiani da **Sangallo il Giovane** *(Sangallo the Younger)*, 1483–1546
– **Tiziano** Vecellio *(Titian)*, 1490–1576
– Jacopo di Robusti, known as **il Tintoretto** *(Tintoretto)*, 1518–1594

VILLA BORGHESE

The Romans' favourite park is just north of the centre. They come here to cycle, jog, ride horses, play football—or just to daydream in the shade of the green oaks and umbrella pines.

Giardini del Pincio E 1

These magnificent gardens above the Piazza del Popolo were designed by Valadier. The wide, tree-lined alleys are a favourite place of Romans for taking a stroll. At sunset the dome of St Peter's can be seen bathed in a heavenly golden glow.

Giardini di Villa Borghese F 1

There are several approaches to the gardens of the Villa Borghese: through Porta Pinciana at the end of Via Veneto, from the Giardini del Pincio, or the monumental entrance from Piazzale Flaminio.

The huge park was created in 1605 by Cardinal Borghese and became state property in 1902. Within its bounds are museums, galleries, archaeological schools, a zoo, an amphitheatre, an artificial lake, pavilions, fountains, neoclassical statues and fantastic constructions to delight the eye—something for everyone.

Museo Borghese F 1

Villa Borghese
Piazzale del Museo Borghese 5
Daily (except Mon)
9 a.m.–7.30 p.m.

On the ground floor of the villa, the museum comprises a picture gallery and an outstanding private collection of sculpture, including works by Bernini and Canova.

Galleria Nazionale d'Arte Moderna F 1

Villa Borghese
Viale delle Belle Arti 131
Daily (except Mon)
8.30 a.m.–7.30 p.m.;
Sun 9 a.m.–8 p.m.

An important collection of Italian painting and sculpture from the 19th and 20th centuries, with works by Carrà, De Chirico, Modigliani, Boccioni, landscape artists from northern Italy, Tuscan impressionists, and so on.

One section is devoted to foreign artists, for example Cézanne, Monet, Klimt, Kandinsky and Utrillo.

Museo Etrusco

Villa Giulia
Piazzale di Villa Giulia 9
(off map, dir. E 1)
Daily (except Mon)
8.30 a.m.–7.30 p.m.

Out of place in a cityscape of domes and ochre stones, the white Vittorio Emanuele Monument on Piazza Venezia commemorates Italian unity.

This museum is just northwest of the modern art gallery. Very little is known of the Etruscans, a mysterious people who came by sea and settled on the peninsula in about 900 BC. The ancient Romans destroyed all traces of them, but objects exhumed from their burial sites reveal an attractive culture. Villa Giulia houses the most important Etruscan museum in Italy: on display is the famous Sarcofago degli Sposi (a tomb sculpted like a couch with a reclining married couple), statuettes, gold jewellery and kitchen utensils.

Catacombs of Priscilla

Catacombe di Priscilla
Via Salaria Nuova 430
(off map dir. G 1)
Daily (except Mon)
8.30 a.m.–noon and
2.30–5 p.m. (5.30 p.m. in summer)
Near Villa Ada, these 2nd-century catacombs are on two levels. They are named after a Roman lady from a family of senators who converted to Christianity in the 1st century. Two painted stuccoes illustrate *The Good Shepherd* and *The Last Supper*. The "Greek Chapel" is decorated with niches, water features and other ornaments.

QUIRINAL AND EAST OF CENTRE

This is the modern city of banks, insurance companies, embassies and high-class hotels, spreading from the Via Veneto to the Baths of Diocletian. The Quirinal Hill is the highest of Rome's famous seven; at the top is the residence of the Italian President.

Piazza Barberini F 2

In the centre of the square stands one of Bernini's most beautiful fountains, the **Fontana del Tritone**, erected in 1642 for Pope Urban VIII Barberini: four dolphins support a great scallop shell on which a Triton is spouting water through a conch shell. Another lovely fountain by Bernini is hidden in a corner of the same square, at the foot of Via Veneto. The **Fontana delle Api** is a scallop shell from which three huge bees are drinking.

Piazza del Quirinale F 3

This square is enhanced by the beautiful *Fontana di Monte Cavallo*. Its statues of Castor and Pollux and their horses were taken from the Baths of Constantine (4th century). The basin of the fountain was previously in the Forum, where it was used as a water trough until 1813. The obelisk comes from the Mausoleum of Augustus. The **Palazzo del Quirinale** (open Sundays) is an imposing complex begun in 1730, the work of several great architects including Domenico Fontana, Carlo Maderno and Bernini. First the summer palace of the Popes, then the Royal Palace, it became the official residence of the President of the Republic in 1947.

Giardini di Villa Aldobrandini F 3

⋮ Via Mazzarino 1

This state-owned villa is closed to the public but you can wander at will in the gardens, which provide a haven of peace in the city centre, criss-crossed by gravel walks with inviting benches.

Museo Nazionale delle Paste Alimentari F 3

⋮ Piazza Scanderbeg 117
⋮ Tel. 06 6991119
⋮ Daily 9.30 a.m.–5.30 p.m.

A unique museum devoted to pasta in all shapes and sizes, from its hand-rolled origins to modern mass-produced spaghetti.

Sant'Andrea al Quirinale F 3

⋮ Via del Quirinale 29

A jewel of baroque architecture, this elliptical church was designed

BERNINI'S ROME

Naples-born Gian Lorenzo Bernini (1598–1680) gives the lie to the opinion that nice guys don't make great geniuses. This cheerful, good-hearted fellow learned his craft from his sculptor-father and was equally happy to pass on his knowledge to disciples. The warmth of his character is evident in the exuberance of his sculpture and in the grace and nobility of his architecture.

A 2-hour walk takes in his major works. Departure point is the church of **Santa Maria della Vittoria** (which includes the Cornaro chapel) on Largo Santa Susanna (G 2), northwest of Termini railway station. Follow Via Barberini until you reach Piazza Barberini, with its two **fountains**. Turn into Via delle Quattro Fontane to see the **Palazzo Barberini** (F 2). At the next crossroads, walk past the church of San Carlo alle Quattro Fontane (designed by Bernini's rival Borromini) and follow Via del Quirinale (F 3). Admire the long wing of the **Palazzo Quirinale** and the façade of the exquisite church of **Sant'Andrea al Quirinale**, one of Bernini's greatest achievements.

Climb the stairase to Via della Dataria and Vicolo Scanderberg, which leads to a little square of the same name (come back another time to visit the Pasta Museum, see p. 31), then to Vicolo dei Modelli, where the artists' models used to wait to be hired. You arrive at the Trevi Fountain (E 3), which was not designed by Bernini but still reveals the influence he exerted on Roman architectural taste. Leave the square by Via delle Muratte and, at the end of the street, turn right into Via del Corso. You will soon reach Piazza Colonna and the **Palazzo di Montecitorio**, begun by Bernini and now serving as the seat of the Italian parliament.

Via in Aquino leads to the Pantheon. Pope Urban VIII wanted Bernini to redecorate the dome, but the artist refused, declaring that it was perfect as it was. From here, make a small detour to Piazza della Minerva, where a little **elephant** supports a strange obelisk, in front of the church of Santa Maria sopra Minerva.

Retrace your steps, then climb the Salita dei Crescenzi to the splendid **Piazza Navona** (D 3), redesigned by Bernini for Pope Innocent X. He also designed the **Fountain of the Four Rivers**, but the statues were sculpted by other artists; only the central figure of the **Fontana del Moro** is Bernini's own work. His contemporaries were fascinated by the way he modelled rocks, shells and other natural elements, and by his witty use of water.

Push on a little further and you will reach the river banks and the **Ponte Sant'Angelo** (C 3), lined with Bernini's windswept angels. To the left, at the end of Via della Conciliazone, is perhaps his best-known work, the world-embracing **Piazza San Pietro** in front of St Peter's Basilica with the tombs of the popes, the famous high altar and the bronze baldacchino (canopy).

by Bernini and built by his assistants between 1658 and 1670 for the novices of the Society of Jesus. Paintings by Baciccia adorn the chapels. The ornate cupola symbolizes a heaven inhabited by chubby cherubs swinging on garlands. The high altar, surrounded by columns of pink marble, is crowned by a golden cupola where clouds of little angels cling to rays of light apparently springing from heaven.

Giant bees have escaped from the Barberini family crest to drink their fill from the Fontana delle Api.

San Carlo alle Quattro Fontane F 3

Via del Quirinale 23

This masterpiece by Borromini is dedicated to Saint Carlo Borromeo. A riot of curves, and very beautiful, it is known affectionately as "San Carlino" because of its small size.

Piazza della Repubblica G 2–3

Mario Rutelli created a scandal in 1901 with his Fontana delle Naiadi placed outside the church of Santa Maria degli Angeli. It is

URBANVS VIII PONTIFEX MAXIMVS
PONTIFI AD PVBLICVM VRBIS ORNAMENTVM
EXSTRVCIO
SINGVLORVM VSIBVS SEORSIM COMMODITATE AC
CONSVLVIT
ANNO MDCXLIV PONT XXI

adorned with four nude bronze naiads, each reclining on an animal: a water snake representing rivers, a swan symbolizing lakes, a lizard for underground streams and a sea horse for the oceans. In the centre, the sea god Glaucos clasps a dolphin.

Santa Maria degli Angeli e dei Martiri G 2

Via Cernaia 9

Incorporated into the ruins of the Baths of Diocletian, this church is dedicated to the angels and the Christian martyrs employed in the building of the baths. Designed by Michelangelo, it was greatly modified by Luigi Vanvitelli in 1749. See the *Martyrdom of Saint Sebastian* by Zampieri and the statue of Saint Bruno by Jean-Antoine Houdon.

Museo Nazionale Romano G 2

Terme di Diocleziano
Via de Nicola 79
Daily (except Mon)
9 a.m.–6.45 p.m.; Sun and holidays 9 a.m.–7.40 p.m., sometimes later in summer

Part of the ruins of the Baths of Diocletian, the museum displays major collections of stucco, frescoes, mosaics and sculpture from the various excavations in Rome since 1870.

Palazzo Massimo alle Terme G 2

Largo di Villa Peretti, 1
Daily 9 a.m.–7.45 p.m., sometimes later in summer

A Jesuit college built in the 19th century, the palace was restored over 16 years and opened in 1998 as part of the Museo Nazionale Romano. The ground and first floors are devoted to sculpture.

In room VII, look for the beautiful Greek *Niobide*, a young girl trying to pull out an arrow piercing her back. In room V is a pretty crouching *Aphrodite*. Coins and gold are displayed in the basement, but it is well worth taking the guided tours of the top two floors, where you can see, among other splendours, the dining room *(triclinium)* of Livia's villa (30–20 BC), decorated with frescoes and mosaics, and even more frescoes from a Roman mansion discovered in the Trastevere district when part of the river below the Villa Farnesina was drained.

Piazza del Cinquecento G–H 3

A column of light, the *Obelisco di luce*, was erected in the square at the beginning of the year 2000, making a luminous welcome for the millions of millennium visitors arriving at the Termini railway station.

Santa Maria Maggiore G 3

⋮ Piazza di Santa Maria Maggiore

The different architectural styles of this basilica mingle harmoniously. Inside, the 40 columns and three naves date from the 5th century. Pope Gregory XI had the bell tower constructed on his return from Avignon in 1377. The caisson ceiling was installed during the Renaissance; the two cupolas and the baroque façade are from the 18th century. The site of the church was designated by Pope Liberius, to whom the Virgin Mary appeared in a dream, ordering him to build a church where he found snow. In the middle of a torrid Roman summer, on August 5, 356, it snowed on the Esquiline Hill.

Santa Prassede G 4

⋮ Via Santa Prassede

Pope Paschal I had the remains of 2,000 martyrs removed from the catacombs and buried here, on the site of a 5th-century church. St Prassede was the daughter of a Roman Senator who gave shelter to Saint Peter. The Chapel of St Zeno in the right-hand nave, covered in golden mosaics, was built on the orders of the same pope as a mausoleum for his mother Theodora.

DEPARTMENT STORES AND SHOPPING CENTRES

Rome doesn't have many department stores, giving the preference to specialized shops. However, you could spend a few hours looking around **La Rinascente**; the branch on piazza Colonna (E 3) was Rome's first department store, inaugurated in 1887. It's open every day, Sundays too, from 9.30 a.m. to 10 p.m. There's an even bigger Rinascente, with yet more choice, same hours, on Piazza Fiume (G 1). On Via Mantova (H 1), just north of Piazzale Porta Pia, **COIN** is a magnificent department store specializing in clothing, lingerie, beauty products and perfume, set in the premises of a former brewery. The second branch of COIN is behind San Giovanni in Laterano, on Piazzale Appio 7.

Close to Cinecittà, on Via Tuscolana on the southeastern edge of the city, **Centro Commerciale Cinecittà Due** is a newish shopping centre grouping a hundred stores and boutiques, as well as numerous bars, banks and restaurants. You can get there on the metro, line A. At the terminus of metro line B, Laurentina, is an even bigger shopping centre, **I Granai**.

The main chain stores are **Standa** (mainly food; branches at Via Cola di Rienzo 173, Viale Trastevere 60 and Via Appia Nuova 181–3) and **UPIM** (Via del Tritone 172, Via Nazionale 211, Piazza Santa Maria Maggiore 5/E). They sell clothing and a range of household goods, all at reasonable prices.

TRASTEVERE

In ancient times, foreigners and immigrants settled in this area "across the Tiber", and in the Middle Ages it was the Jewish quarter. A traditional working-class area full of winding alleyways, quaint shops and smart art galleries, it is certainly worth exploring.

Galleria Corsini C 4
(Galleria Nazionale
d'Arte Antica)

: Palazzo Corsini
: Via della Lungara 10
: Daily (except Mon)
: 8.30 a.m.–7.30 p.m.

Over the centuries, many distinguished people have stayed in the Corsini Palace—Michelangelo, Bramante, Erasmus and Queen Christina of Sweden, who died here. It contains a large collection of 17th- and 18th-century paintings by Lippi, Raphael, Bronzino, Caravaggio, Holbein, Rubens, Van Dyck and more.

Villa Farnesina D 4

: Via della Lungara 230
: Mon–Sat 9 a.m.–1 p.m.

The wealthy banker Agostino Chigi had this beautiful Renaissance house built by the Siennese architect Baldassare Peruzzi from 1508. Peruzzi also decorated some of the rooms, notably the Sala delle Prospettive, painted in trompe-l'œil to give the illusion of a loggia open to the Roman countryside. Most of the frescoes, however, are the work of Raphael (*The Triumph of Galatea* in the Sala Galatea) or his pupils (*Cupid and Psyche* in the Loggia di Psiche). The villa is surrounded by magnificent gardens.

Santa Maria in Trastevere D 5

: Piazza Santa Maria in Trastevere

This church was probably the first official place of Christian worship built in Rome, dating from the 3rd century. The façade bears a 12th–14th century mosaic of the Virgin and Child with ten maidens. In the apse, mosaics by Pietro Cavallini illustrate six episodes of the life of the Virgin.

Santa Cecilia in Trastevere E 5

: Piazza di Santa Cecilia

Saint Cecilia's church is built on the supposed site of her home; she was martyred at the same time as her husband Valerian. The mosaics in the apse were created after 1143. Opposite the altar, a statue by Stefano Maderno (17th century) shows the saint in the position where her body was found, miraculously intact, in the catacombs of San Callisto. Pietro

Since ancient times Rome has refreshed its air with fountains. These cherubs enjoy a shower on Piazza Mastai.

Cavallini's fresco of the *Last Judgment* was discovered in 1900 during restoration work.

San Pietro in Montorio C 5
: Piazza San Pietro in Montorio 2
: Via Garibaldi 33
A Gothic rose window adorns the façade of this building financed by Ferdinand of Aragon and Isabella of Castille. The two chapels were decorated by pupils of Michelangelo. In the centre of the cloister stands an elegant circular temple (Tempietto) by Bramante (1502), located on the supposed site of Saint Peter's crucifixion.

Fontana dell'Acqua Paola C 5
: Via Garibaldi
This fine fountain is shaped like a triumphal arch surmounted by dragons, with monsters in the lateral niches. The three arches give onto a quiet garden.

Parco del Gianicolo C 4–5
This large park occupies the top of the Janiculum Hill, offering a splendid panorama of the city. In the middle of the esplanade stands an imposing statue of Garibaldi. There are pony rides and puppet shows, monuments, fountains and a botanical garden.

THE VATICAN

The Vatican State includes St Peter's Square and Basilica, the Papal palaces and gardens. A thousand people live here, all employed by the Vatican.

In the middle of the 9th century, Pope Leo IV built a wall around the Vatican Hill to protect the basilica that had been built by Constantine over the tomb of Saint Peter. This "Leonine" city corresponds to the modern Vatican City. After 1377, having left Avignon, the Popes took up residence in the Apostolic Palaces, which had grown over the centuries to a complex of 1,400 rooms, chambers and chapels.

To obtain an audience or take part in ceremonies in the Vatican Basilica, you must present a written request to the Prefettura della Casa Pontificia – 00120 Città del Vaticano. Audiences are held every Wednesday (when the Pope is in Rome), generally at 11 a.m.

Castel Sant'Angelo C 2
: Lungotevere Castello 50
: Open daily (except Mon)
: 9 a.m.–7 p.m.,
: sometimes later in summer

Built in AD 139 as a mausoleum for the Emperor Hadrian, this fortress became successively an outpost of the Aurelian Wall, a citadel, a medieval prison and a residence of the Popes (who linked it to the Vatican by building the passetto, a passage in the walls). It was named Sant'Angelo by Pope Gregory the Great who, while riding in a procession during an epidemic of plague, had a vision of the Archangel Saint Michael replacing his sword in its sheath. This was interpreted as a sign that the plague was coming to an end. The Castel is now home to the National Museum: exploring its 58 rooms you retrace the entire history of the building, which also houses collections of ceramics, ancient weapons, paintings and decorative items.

Ponte Sant'Angelo, the bridge which spans the Tiber in front of the Castel, is one of the most handsome in the city. The ten baroque angels in white marble, their robes blowing in the wind, were designed by Gian Lorenzo Bernini and sculpted by Roman artists under his guidance. Each one bears an instrument of Christ's martyrdom. The Recording Angel was sculpted largely by Bernini himself: his two other angels, judged by the Pope as too precious to be exposed to the elements, were placed in the church of Sant'Andrea delle Fratte.

St Peter's Square B 2–3

Piazza San Pietro

From Sant'Angelo, the Via della Conciliazione leads directly to this magnificent square, built between 1656 and 1667 by Bernini. Oval in shape, the square is 240 m (787 ft) wide and 196 m (643 ft) long, watched over by 140 stone saints and surrounded by four rows of columns (284 in all). To see the columns dissolve into a single row, stand on one of the two discs set in the ground half-way between the obelisk and the fountains.

The obelisk was brought from Alexandria to ornament the ancient Circus of Caligula which stood to the left of the present basilica. It was moved to the centre of St Peter's Square in 1586, an operation which took four months and required the efforts of 900 men, 47 cranes and 150 horses. The cross on the top is believed to contain a fragment of the True Cross.

St Peter's Basilica B 3

San Pietro in Vaticano
Piazza San Pietro
Open daily 7 a.m.–6 p.m.;
Sun 8 a.m.–4.45 p.m.

Saint Peter was put to death in the Circus of Caligula in the year 64. In the 2nd century, a sanctuary was erected around his tomb in the necropolis north of the Circus. Constantine built a great basilica on the same site, which was completed in about 349. It was falling into ruin by 1506 when Pope Julius II laid the foundation stone of a new building. This took more than a century to complete, with all the great Renaissance and baroque artists contributing to the work. The vastness of the basilica is difficult to imagine. It measures 187 m (613 ft) in length and contains 11 chapels, 45 altars and countless works of art. Bronze markers in the floor show the dimensions of other great churches, all inferior to St Peter's, of course. The two lateral naves, 76 m (249 ft) long, end under the enormous dome by Michelangelo. One of the same artist's most beautiful works, the marble sculpture of the *Pietà*, which he completed before the age of 25, is in a chapel near the entrance, protected by a glass screen. Bernini's extravagant bronze baldacchino above the high altar is as tall as the Palazzo Farnese.

There is access from the basilica to the Vatican Grottoes, long galleries (still largely unexplored) of painted tombs. You can also take the lift to the Loggia degli Apostoli and then climb the steps to enjoy the view from the terrace.

Vatican Museums B 2

Musei Vaticani
Entrance by a spiral ramp on the right-hand side of St Peter's Square
Mon–Fri and last Sun of month (free entrance) from 8.45 a.m.; closing time varies from 1.45 to 4.45 p.m. depending on the season.
Sat 8.45 a.m.–1.45 p.m.
Closed on national and religious holidays.

The Renaissance palaces built by Popes Sixtus IV, Innocent VII and Julius II house one of the most important art collections in the world. The courtyards and galleries were designed by Bramante in 1503. The later extensions date from the 18th century, when for the first time the priceless works of art were put on public view. You have to follow one of the four colour-coded routes, all of which pass through the Sistine Chapel.
The shortest lasts 90 minutes, the longest (not for the faint-hearted) takes 5 hours. Concentrate on one collection and to plan for short breaks to give your feet—and your brain—a rest. Following is a selection, in alphabetical order.

St Peter's Basilica somehow has the effect of making you feel small.

Borgia Apartments

Appartamenti Borgia
Frescoes by Pinturicchio, portraits of famous Borgias, bronzes by Rodin, ceramics by Picasso, and more.

Chapel of Nicolas V

Cappella del Beato Angelico
Luminous frescoes by Fra Angelico illustrate the lives of Saint Stephen and Saint Laurence.

Chiaramonti Museum

Greek and Roman statuary.

Christian Museum

Museo Pio Cristiano
Works from the catacombs depicting the lives of the early Christians.

Gregorian Egyptian Museum

Museo Gregoriano Egizio
Egyptian pieces from temples and gardens in and around Rome, including copies from Hadrian's villa at Tivoli.

Gregorian Etruscan Museum

Museo Gregoriano Etrusco
Etruscan sarcophagi, statues, bronzes, pottery, glassware and jewellery from the 7th century BC.

Gregorian Profane Museum

Museo Gregoriano Profano
Greek and Roman antiquities.

Historical Museum
⋮ Museo Storico Vaticano
The history of the Vatican and the Papal States, with a collection of antique "popemobiles".

Missionary Ethnological Museum
⋮ Museo Missionario-Etnologico
Accounts by Catholic missionaries, of social and cultural interest.

Modern Religious Art Collection
⋮ Collezione d'Arte Religiosa
⋮ Moderna
Works by Dali, Kandinski, Klee, Matisse, Modigliani, Picasso, Utrillo and more.

Philatelic and Numismatic Museum
⋮ Museo Filatelico e Numismatico
Postage stamps and coins issued by the Vatican State.

Picture Gallery
⋮ Pinacoteca
Fifteen rooms containing ten centuries of unforgettable paintings: Caravaggio, Domenichino, Giotto, Fra Angelico, Perugino, Leonardo Da Vinci.

Pio-Clementino Museum
Greek and Roman sculpture reclaimed at the time of the demolition of ancient monuments in the 16th century, notably the Laocoon group, dug up in a vineyard on the Esquiline Hill in 1506.

Raphael Rooms
⋮ Stanze di Raffaello
Four rooms decorated by the young Raphael for Pope Julius II. Of particular note is the Signature Room.

Sistine Chapel
⋮ Cappella Sistina
Famous the world over, this chapel owes its name to the pope who first had it built, Sixtus IV. (It is the room the cardinals use when they meet to elect a new pope.) From 1475 onwards, with a vast fund of church money at his disposal, Sixtus commissioned the greatest artists of the time—Pinturicchio, Perugino, Botticelli, Ghirlandaio, Signorelli, Rosselli—to cover the walls with frescoes illustrating the lives of Moses and Jesus Christ.
On Michelangelo's ceiling, more than 300 figures illustrate the creation of mankind. In the centre is the scene of Eve's creation, and just next to it, perhaps the best-known image, where God stretches out a finger to create Adam. It was Pope Julius II who persuaded the sculptor to take on this task.

Unfamiliar with fresco techniques, Michelangelo was reluctant to accept the challenge posed by the ceiling's enormous dimensions and its vaulted shape. The resulting masterpiece to prove that he was on a par with the greatest artists of his time. He soon fired his assistants as incompetent, and spent four uncomfortable years, from 1508 to 1512, completing the majestic fresco, standing precariously on tiptoe on a mobile scaffolding he designed himself, his head craned backwards. Julius II, anxious to see the work completed, hassled him constantly, threatening to topple him down from the scaffolding if he didn't hurry up. Twenty-three years later, at the age of 60, Michelangelo began work on the *Last Judgement,* covering the wall behind the high altar. It took him another seven years to finish the cataclysmic scene, the action swirling round a stern-faced Christ dispensing justice. The nudity of the figures offended Pope Paul IV who had some of them painted over with wispy veils by Daniele da Volterra. This earned him the nickname il Braghettone, "the pants-maker". Michelangelo incorporated a deformed self-portrait into the painting: look at the flayed skin held by Saint Bartholomew just below Christ.

Restoration of the Sistine Chapel was begun almost by accident in 1979. During a routine clean-up of the frescoes, someone scratched a corner of the ceiling and noticed the brilliant colours hidden beneath a thick layer of dust and greasy soot from centuries of candles. A detailed inspection revealed that cracks had been caused by the application of glues in preceding restorations.

Financed by the Japanese television company NTV, which was granted the rights to film the entire venture, the restoration took the Vatican's team 13 years to complete.

A special mixture of fungicide, ammonium bicarbonate and sodium bicarbonate was applied to dissolve the impurities, which were then carefully wiped off with a sterilized natural sponge. The result was controversial, as most people were taken aback at the vibrance of colours and the clear outlines of the figures. Sit on a bench near the chapel exit to best judge it for yourself.

Vatican Library
: Biblioteca Apostolica

One million rare books and ancient manuscripts, including a 4th century Gospel of Saint Matthew and a text by Luther, are kept in the library's frescoed halls.

EXCURSIONS

When you can't face another painting and you're suffering from an overload of golden cherubs, take the metro or a train and get out of the city centre.

Cimitero Acattolico
- Via Caio Cestio 6
- (off map dir. E 6)
- Metro Line B to Piramide
- Tues–Sun 9 a.m.–5.30 p.m. in summer; 8 a.m.–3 p.m. in winter

Spread out at the foot of the marble-faced Cestius Pyramid (the mausoleum of praetor Caius Cestus), this cemetery (also called Cimitero Protestante) is one of the most romantic places in Rome. Beneath the dark shade of pines and cypresses, in the company of many other "non-Catholics" (i.e. Protestants, Orthodox, atheists and so on, who were not admitted to the Catholic cemeteries), lie the English poets Keats and Shelley, Goethe's only son, and Antonio Gramsci, founder of the Italian communist party, who died just after being released from eight years of imprisonment.

Testaccio
- Between via Marmorata and the river
- (off map dir. E 6)
- Metro Line B to Piramide

In ancient times, cargoes of wine, oil and wheat were delivered to Rome in clay amphoras, which were emptied, smashed up and the shards thrown onto a dump. The dump grew into a 35-m-high hill, Monte Testaccio, where the Romans built a marble warehouse. At the end of the 19th century the Testaccio became a working-class neighbourhood, clustered around a slaughterhouse. It has now developed into an entertainment centre, with friendly restaurants and a lively nightlife. Bars and discotheques have been gouged out of the side of the hill, and you can still make out the odd fragment of amphora embedded in the walls.

Art Center Acea
- Centrale Montemartini
- Via Ostiense 106
- (off map dir. E 6)
- Metro Line B to Piramide or Garbatella
- Daily (except Mon) 9.30 a.m.–7 p.m.

A fascinating exhibition called "Machines and Gods": it consists of 400 marble statues from the Capitoline museums, placed in the unlikely setting of generators, tubing and boilers in a disused power station.

San Paolo Fuori le Mura

Via Ostiense 186
(off map dir. E 6)
Metro Line B to Basilica S. Paolo

The Church of St Paul's Outside the Walls is a faithful reconstruction of the great 4th century basilica devastated by fire in 1823. There is a splendid Venetian mosaic (1220) in the apse. Under the altar is the tomb of Saint Paul, believed to be buried here although several other places claim the same honour. The cloister, built in 1208 and spared by the flames, is one of the finest in Rome. In the centre is a charming rose garden.

EUR (Esposizione Universale di Roma)

Metro Line B to Marconi or Fermi
5 km south

Begun on the orders of Mussolini, for a Universal Exposition that never took place because of World War II, this district of glassy office blocks and stark apartment buildings has some interesting examples of monumental Fascist architecture and several museums.
The **Museo della Civiltà romana**, piazza G. Agnelli (Tues–Sat 9 a.m.– 6.45 p.m.; Sun 9 a.m.–1.30 p.m.) traces the history of Rome. Its highlight is a scale model of the imperial city, depicting every building inside the Aurelian Wall.

The **Museo nazionale preistorico ed etnografico Luigi Pigorini**, on the corner of piazza Marconi and viale Lincoln (daily 9 a.m.– 8 p.m.) studies the people of the world. There's also a collection of local prehistoric finds.
The **Museo nazionale delle Arti e Tradizioni popolari** on the other side of Piazza Marconi (Tues–Sun 9 a.m.–6 p.m.) illustrates Italian customs and traditions, displaying household utensils and agricultural tools, pottery, jewellery and other objects garnered from villages.

Castelli Romani

Metro Line A to Anagnina, then bus to the various localities (trips from 30 min to 1 1/2 hr).
12 km (7 miles) southeast

In the Middle Ages, a number of castles were built in the foothills of the Colli Albani: these eventually became fortified villages and then developed into small hill towns. This is where modern Romans spend their weekends. You will be spoilt for choice: Frascati and its splendid villas, in particular Villa Aldobrandini; Castel Gandolfo, the summer residence of the Pope; Ariccia with its baroque palaces by Bernini; Genzano, famous for the Corpus Domini festival in June when a carpet of flowers covers the

steps up to the church of Santa Maria della Cima; Rocca di Papa; Monte Compatri, and many others.

Fregene
: Metro Line A to Lepanto, then bus to Fregene (1 hr).
: 30 km (19 miles) from Rome
An elegant resort by the sea, surrounded by greenery.

Ostia Antica
: Metro Line B to Magliana, then train to Ostia (30 min).
: 25 km (16 miles) southwest
This used to be the main commercial port of Rome, abandoned because of malaria. The ancient city was buried under sand for centuries.

Tivoli
: Metro Line B to Rebibbia then COTRAL bus to Tivoli (45 min).
: 31 km (19 miles) from Rome
This is where the ancient Romans used to spend their holidays. You can stroll in the gardens of splendid villas: Villa d'Este with its grottoes and fountains; Villa Gregoriana and its tree-filled garden; and Villa Adriana, a vast open-air museum illustrating all the ostentation of the Roman Empire.

A carpet of flowers, well-watered for Corpus Domini.

Dining Out

In the restaurants and trattorie listed here you can eat well without burning a hole in your pocket. Roman pizzas are as good as those in Naples, their home town. The *pizzerie* are generally open evenings only, when the wood fires are lit to give this delicious speciality its characteristic flavour. If you're just looking for a snack, try an *enoteche*, or wine bar, which serves local specialities as well as wine. Bars and cafés also sell delicious sandwiches, hot toasted *panini* and irresistible pastries. There's nowhere better for a short rest and the chance to observe Rome's *dolce vita*.

The restaurants are listed in alphabetical order, under subheadings corresponding to the sightseeing section of this guide.

ANCIENT ROME

Agustarello a Testaccio
Via G. Branca 98
(off map dir. E 6)
Tel. 06 574 65 85
Closed Sun, and Mon lunch
North of Monte Testaccio in the old part of town, this is a fine restaurant serving traditional Roman specialities.

Apuleius E 6
Via Tempio di Diana 15
Tel. 06 574 21 60
Closed Sat lunch and Sun
The décor of this typical tavern in the heart of the Aventino district will plunge you into the atmosphere of ancient Rome. Hidden away in an overgrown wall.

HISTORIC CENTRE

Achilli al Parlamento E 3
Via dei Prefetti 15
Tel. 06 687 34 46
Closed Sun, and Mon lunch
An *enoteche* or wine bar offering delicious canapés, a cold buffet and a variety of tarts and pies to accompany a glass or two of excellent Italian wine.

AL 34 E 2
Via Mario de' Fiori 34
Tel. 06 679 50 91
Closed Mon
Near Piazza di Spagna—the ideal place for a romantic tête-à-tête. The cuisine is excellent, proposing a menu of out-of-the-ordinary specialities.

Al Pompiere D 3
- Via Santa Maria dei Calderari 38
- Tel. 06 686 83 77
- Closed Sun

In the Cenci Palace, at the heart of the Jewish Ghetto, this restaurant serves classic dishes. There's a huge dining room on the first floor, with a painted ceiling. Don't forget to save some room for the ricotta and plum tart.

Alla Corte dei Borboni E 1
- Via di Ripetta 43/44
- Tel. 06 360 046 81

Traditional Neapolitan cuisine brought to the heart of Rome.

Antico Caffè Greco E 2
- Via Condotti 86
- Tel. 06 67 917 00

Liszt, Gogol, Goethe and many other celebrities have frequented this café which was founded in 1760.

Antico Caffè della Pace D 3
- Via della Pace 3–7
- Tel. 06 686 12 16
- Closed Mon morning.

Traditional café north of Piazza Navona frequented by writers and artists, always filled with smoke. Delicious chocolate desserts.

Antica Enoteca E 2
- Via della Croce 76
- Tel. 06 679 08 96
- Closed in August

A delightfully old-fashioned wine bar and restaurant with good, down-to-earth Roman cooking; one

---

A MENU "ALLA ROMANA"

Begin your meal with some delicious *bruschette* (toasted bread rubbed with garlic and oil) served as a starter. Then comes the pasta: *bucatini all'amatriciana* or *spaghetti alla carbonara*. Next, the main course of meat, often served with vegetables: *coda alla vaccinara* (oxtail), *abbacchio al forno* (baked lamb), *scottadito* (lamb chops), *saltimbocca alla romana* (thin slices of veal with ham and sage). Don't miss the *carciofi* (artichokes) prepared *alla romana* or *alla giudia*.

Room for dessert? Try the wonderful *tiramisù*, the *crostate alla ricotta*, and of course the home-made ice cream.

As for wines, the best-known Roman white is Frascati, but Castelli Romani, Marino, Colli Albani, Velletri and Verdicchio are also very drinkable. The reds often come from other regions of Italy: Chianti, Barolo, Dolcetto, Rosso di Montalcino and Montepulciano. House wines are often surprisingly good drinking.

of the most sought-out establishments in Rome. It also sells olive oil and *grappa* (a fiery spirit made from grape must).

Antica Enoteca Beccaria D 1
- Via C. Beccaria 14
- Tel. 06 321 73 57
- Closed Sat afternoon

Off Piazzale Flaminio, a few tables and a bar for sampling Italian wine, cheese, salami and *porchetto*.

Babington's Tea Rooms F 6
- Piazza di Spagna 23
- Tel. 06 678 60 27
- Closed Tues

Founded by two English ladies over 100 years ago, it still serves real English tea, scones and crumpets.

Bar del Fico D 3
- Piazza del Fico 26/28
- Tel. 06 686 52 05
- Closed Sun morning

A trendy clientele of actors, artists, politicians and bigwigs who put the world to rights under the superb fig tree.

Bottega del Vino da Bleve D 3
- Via S. Maria del Pianto 9/49
- Tel. 06 686 59 70
- Closed Sun and Mon

Friendly restaurant near the Campo dei Fiori with efficient service. No-nonsense tasty fare.

Caffè Farnese D 4
- Via dei Baullari 106
- Tel. 06 688 021 25

Well-placed near Piazza Farnese for watching the world go by.

La Campana E 3
- Vicolo della Campana
- Tel. 06 686 78 20
- Closed Mon

A historic, 150-year-old trattoria in a 16th-century palace near Montecitorio. Excellent quality

Il Cardinale D 4
- Via delle Carceri 6
- Tel. 06 687 84 30

An elegant restaurant in an ancient palace near Via Giulia.

Ciampini al Café du Jardin E 2
- Piazza Trinità dei Monti 1
- Tel. 06 678 56 78
- Closed Wed, end Nov to end Feb

The perfect place to sip your evening apéritif or eat a delicious ice cream as you watch the sun set over the Eternal City. It's at the top of the Spanish Steps, with a roof garden and restaurant.

Corallo D 3
- Via del Corallo 10
- Tel. 06 683 077 03
- Daily 7 p.m.–1 a.m.

West of Piazza Navona, a wide selection of pizzas and *focacce*.

Cul de Sac F 7

: Piazza Pasquino 73
: Tel. 06 688 010 94

Wine bar near Piazza Navona offering wines from every region of Italy and a wide selection of gastronomic delights: smoked meats, bean soup, desserts.

Da Baffetto D 3

: Via del Governo Vecchio 114
: Tel. 06 686 16 17
: Evenings only

Enormous pizzas, on a busy corner of Piazza Navona.

Ditirambo D 4

: Piazza della Cancelleria 74
: Tel. 06 687 16 26
: Closed Mon lunch

Pleasant and well-kept trattoria. Give your preference to dishes prepared with vegetables in season.

Gelateria della Palma E 3

: Via della Maddalena 23
: Tel. 06 688 067 52.

Exquisite ices. It's absolutely agonizing to have to choose from the 100 flavours on offer.

Giolitti E 3

: Via degli Uffici del Vicario 40
: Tel. 06 699 12 43

A famous *gelateria* near Piazza di Montecitorio proposing fabulous ice cream concoctions. Greedy gourmets will appreciate the gigantic *Torre Eiffel* (Eiffel Tower, almost as big) house speciality, not to mention the *Coppa Olimpica Mondiale.*

Il Gusto E 2

: Piazza Augusto Imperatore 9
: Via della Frezza 23
: Tel. 06 322 62 73

This is not only a restaurant, pizzeria and wine bar, but also a bookshop and library devoted to wine, and a shop selling all sorts of gourmet gifts and regional products. Just north of Mausoleo di Augusto.

La Bevitoria D 3

: Piazza Navona 72
: Tel. 06 688 010 22

Italian wines, snacks and other appetizers.

La Penna d'Oca E 1

: Via della Penna 53
: Tel. 06 320 28 98
: Evenings only

Mainly fish, but the menu includes meat dishes, too, and home-made cakes for dessert.

La Taverna di Giovanni D 3

: Via del Banco di Santo Spirito 58
: Tel. 06 686 41 16
: Closed Mon

Opposite Castel Sant'Angelo, all the best Roman specialities: *rigatoni all'amatriciana, gnocchi, tripa...*

La Trinchetta D 3
- Via dei Banchi Nuovi 4
- Tel. 06 683 001 33
- Closed Sun lunch

Imaginative cuisine and excellent wines.

Mare et Vino D 3
- Via dei Sediari 2
- Tel. 06 686 93 36
- Closed Sun

Tranquil setting in the midst of narrow streets, excellent cuisine,

especially the spaghetti named after the restaurant, "sea and wine".

Margutta Vegetariano E 1
- Via Margutta 111
- Tel. 06 326 505 77.

If you're a vegetarian and feel as though you're condemned to eating pizzas, look no further. Home-made pasta with a vegetable sauce, veggie hamburgers, aubergine cutlets and other inspired dishes.

Osteria dell'Antiquario D 3
- Piazzetta San Simeone 26
- Tel. 06 687 96 94
- Closed Sun

A creative chef who knows how to adapt traditional dishes to modern tastes… but quite expensive.

Otello alla Concordia E 2
- Via della Croce 81
- Tel. 06 679 11 78
- Closed Sun

A restaurant specializing in fish dishes, in a 17th-century palace with garden.

Pancrazio D 3
- Piazza del Biscione 92
- Tel. 06 686 12 46
- Closed Wed

In summer, you can eat outside at this restaurant built on the ruins of Pompey's Theatre.

A BRIEF HISTORY OF ICE CREAM

Among the many good things Marco Polo is credited with bringing back from China in the 13th century, let us give thanks for ice cream. Actually, he was not the first Italian to dabble in this cold ambrosia. Nero used to serve a delicious concoction of puréed fruits, honey and snow. The undisputed masters of Italian *gelati* at the end of the 18th century were Signori Pratti and Tortoni, who toured the courts of Europe with their frozen delicacies. Then, in the early 20th century, the US laid claim to world supremacy—not long after the first wave of Italians had passed through immigration.

Porto di Ripetta E 1
: Via di Ripetta 250
: Tel. 06 361 23 76
: Closed Sun

Fish prepared in inventive ways, for example, *zuppa di fagioli e pesce* (fish and bean soup) or *gamberoni ai carciofi* (crayfish with artichokes).

Ristorante Ranieri E 2
: Via Mario dei Fiori 26
: Tel. 06 679 33 35
: Closed Sun

One of the oldest restaurants in the capital. Antique furniture and a high standard of service.

Segrestia E 3
: Via del Seminario 89
: Tel. 06 679 75 81
: Closed Wed

Restaurant specializing in classic Roman cuisine.

Sant'Eustachio E 3
: Piazza Sant'Eustachio 82
: Tel. 06 654 20 48

Among the most famous bars in the city, on a pretty piazza near the Pantheon. Its special coffee, *gran caffè,* is said to be the best in Rome.

Settimio all'Arancio E 3
: Via dell'Arancio 50
: Tel. 06 687 61 19
: Closed Sun July and August

Pizzas with unexpected toppings.

Tre Scalini D 3
: Piazza Navona 28–30
: Tel. 06 687 91 48
: Closed Wed

It may be a bit heavy on the wallet, but don't resist the temptation to taste the delicious *tartufo al cioccolato* (chocolate truffle) for which this café is justly famous. Magnificent location on the piazza.

Vecchia Roma E 4
: Piazza Campitelli 18
: Tel. 06 686 46 04
: Closed Wed

A church converted to a restaurant, north of Teatro di Marcello. Outside terrace in fine weather. Imaginative summer salads, good risottos and pasta year round.

QUIRINALE AND EAST OF CENTRE

Al Boschetto F 3
: Via del Boschetto 30
: Tel. 06 474 47 70
: Closed Sat lunch

A rustic-style trattoria where you can enjoy unusual pasta and meat dishes.

Al Ceppo
: Via Panama 2
: (off map dir. G 1)
: Tel. 06 855 13 79
: Closed Mon

Elegant but prices are reasonable. Roman cooking, excellent grilled meat dishes and desserts that are not to be missed. Stop by on your way to the Catacombs of Priscilla.

Al Moro F 3
- Vicolo delle Bollette 13
- Tel. 06 678 34 95
- Closed Sun

A trattoria offering plain and simple food in a boisterous atmosphere.

Alfredo a Via Gabi H 6
- Via Gabi 36
- Tel. 06 772 067 92
- Closed Tues

A large trattoria with a pergola behind San Giovanni in Laterano. Rich food and copious servings: try the pasta with mushrooms in a cream sauce or the *straccetti al gorgonzola*: finely sliced beef in a cheese sauce.

Andrea F 1
- Via Sardegna 26/28
- Tel. 06 482 18 91
- Closed Sat lunch and Sun

A vast choice of hors-d'œuvres and for a special treat, delicious lobster to follow.

Arancia blu
- Via dei Latini 65
- (off map dir. H 3)
- Tel. 06 445 41 05

Open every evening from 8.30 p.m. Reservation advised. Imagnative vegetarion cuisine for wine connoisseurs.

Bonne Nouvelle F 4
- Via del Boschetto 73
- Tel. 06 486 781
- Closed Sun

Simple, elegant, welcoming. Very good fish dishes.

Café de Paris F 1
- Via Vittorio Veneto 90
- Tel. 06 581 53 78

The meeting place for the *dolce vita*, and a great favourite with visitors.

Cannavota H 5–6
- Piazza San Giovanni in Laterano 20
- Tel. 06 772 050 07
- Closed Wed

The cooking is reliable and the portions generous. Let yourself be tempted by the crayfish. Popular with the locals.

Cantina Cantarini H 1
- Piazza Sallustio 12
- Tel. 06 485 528
- Closed Sun

Near Porta Pia, an unforgettable *fritto misto* and a friendly atmosphere. From Thurs evening to Sat, fish from the Adriatic.

Cesarina G 1
: Via Piemonte 109
: Tel. 06 488 08 28
: Closed Sun

Specialities from Rome but also from the Emilia-Romagna district in Northern Italy, with good fish dishes.

Da Franco ar Vicoletto
: Via dei Falisci 1
: (off map dir. H 3)
: Tel. 06 495 76 75
: Closed Mon

The freshest of fish prepared in many original and delectable ways.

Est! Est!! Est!!! G 3
: Via Genova 32
: Tel. 06 488 11 07
: Closed Mon

This is one of Rome's best-known pizzerias, on the street between the Via Nazionale and the Ministry of the Interior. Soak up the jovial atmosphere while you sample a *calzoni* (folded pizza) or the *filetti di baccalà* (cod fillets).

Goffredo da Robertino F 4
: Via Panisperna 231
: Tel. 06 474 06 20
: Closed Mon

Classic yet inventive cooking in an establishment that opened in 1886. Champagne risotto, fish and good meat dishes.

Mario's F 4
: Piazza del Grillo 9
: Tel. 06 679 37 25
: Closed Mon

Behind the Foro di Augusto, sophisticated fish dishes, carefully prepared.

TRASTEVERE

Bibli D 5
: Via dei Fienaroli 28
: Tel. 06 581 45 44
: Closed Mon lunch

Appetizing conjunction of bookshop and restaurant.

Checco er Carrettiere D 5
: Via Benedetta 10
: Tel. 06 580 09 85
: Closed Sun evening
: and Mon

A typically Roman restaurant at the end of Ponte Sisto, handed down from father to son for more than 60 years. Fresh fish.

Da Paris D 5
: Piazza San Callisto 7A
: Tel. 06 581 53 78
: Closed Sun evening and Mon

Roman and Jewish cooking. Make sure you have a hearty appetite when you come here, as every course, from the soups, the *fritti misti* to the desserts is a must.

Ivo D 5
- Via di San Francesco a Ripa 158
- Tel. 06 581 70 82
- Closed Tues

In summer, the tables of this pizzeria are set in the street, so you can watch the world go by while you are eating.

La Cornucopia E 5
- Piazza in Piscinula 18
- Tel. 06 580 03 80
- Closed Tues

Romantic atmosphere in this restaurant at the end of Ponte Palatino. In fine weather, you can dine outside by candlelight. Excellent fish.

Romolo nel Giardino della Fornarina D 5
- Via Porta Settimiana 8
- Tel. 06 581 82 84
- Closed Mon

An institution. The dream setting for a candlelight dinner served to the gentle strains of a guitar. The Fornarina of the name was the innkeeper's daughter, mistress of the painter Raphael, who lived here in the 16th century.

Taverna Trilussa D 5
- Via del Politeama 22
- Tel. 06 581 89 18
- Open every evening and also Sun lunch

A very wide choice of succulent pasta dishes, near Ponte Sisto.

VATICAN AREA

L'Angoletto ai Musei B 1
- Via Leone IV 2A
- Tel. 06 397 231 87
- Closed Tues

A very friendly pizzeria handily situated near the Vatican Museums. Good pizzas, both at lunchtime and in the evening.

Lorodinapoli C 1
- Via Fabio Massimo 101
- Tel. 06 323 57 90
- Closed Sun

Authentic Neapolitan cuisine, down to the tiniest details. The menu changes every evening. A popular show-biz venue.

Piero e Francesco C 1
- Via Fabio Massimo 75–77
- Tel. 06 397 207 04
- Closed Sun

Fresh fish served in many imaginative ways. A bit pricey.

Zi Gaetana C 2
- Via Cola di Rienzo 263
- Tél. 321 23 42
- Closed Sun

Pizza and other unpretentious dishes, music, a typically boisterous atmosphere.

Entertainment

The narrow streets around the Trastevere, Piazza Navona, the Pantheon and the Testaccio are the liveliest after sundown, and there are numerous nightclubs around the Via Veneto. To see all the possibilities Rome has to offer, consult publications such as *Città Aperta* and *Roma c'è*, the guide *Time Out Roma* (in English), or the entertainment page or weekly supplement in daily newspapers such as *Il Messaggero*, *Il Manifesto*, *Paese Sera* and *La Repubblica*.

CLASSICAL MUSIC

The concerts of sacred music held in the churches are usually of exceptional quality; programmes are posted all over town. But there's also opera and ballet, plenty to keep you entertained.

Teatro dell'Opera
⋮ Piazza Beniamino Gigli
⋮ Tel. 06 481 601
Well-known operas to sing along with.

Teatro Olimpico
⋮ Piazza Gentile da Fabriano 17
⋮ Tel. 06 326 59 91
Concerts, ballets and chamber music.

Terme di Caracalla
⋮ Viale delle Terme di Caracalla 52
In summer, open-air opera and dance. Reservations at the Teatro dell'Opera.

JAZZ AND ROCK MUSIC

Alexanderplatz
⋮ Via Ostia 9
⋮ Tel. 06 397 421 71
A jazz club with a history. The greatest Italian and international musicians have played here, and left their autographs on the walls to prove it.

Dome Rock Café
⋮ Via della Fontana 18
⋮ Tel. 06 705 24 36
Friendly atmosphere and excellent cocktails in an out-of-the-ordinary setting.

Fonclea
⋮ Via Crescenzio 82A
⋮ Tel. 06 689 63 02
⋮ Open every evening
There's lots of jazz in this popular venue, but also soul music, rock and funk.

Salamandra

: Via Matricardi 22 (Magliana)
: Tel. 06 552 613 12

The accent is on jazz.

BARS AND NIGHTCLUBS

Argonauta

: Lungotevere degli Artigiani

For an evening out with a
difference, come dancing on a boat
moored on the Tiber.

Club 84

: Via Emilia 84
: Tel. 06 482 75 38

A discothèque to get your toes
tapping.

ROME ON THE SCREEN

Classical cinema offers a great
introduction to the Eternal City.
Roberto Rossellini depicts the
war-torn capital of 1945 in Open
City. Pier Paolo Pasolini's Mamma
Roma shows the darker, unsenti-
mental side of proletarian Rome,
with Anna Magnani starring as a
prostitute. But Federico Fellini is
the supreme film chronicler of
modern Rome, from *La Dolce Vita*,
his portrait of the crazy 60s of
playboys, playgirls and paparazzi,
to Fellini Roma, the director's
love-letter to the city of his youth
and his manhood, with all its joys
and all its grotesqueness.

Escopazzo

: Via dell'Aracoeli 41
: Tel. 06 692 004 22

Live music, jam sessions and a well-
stocked bar where you can make
your way through 200 different
cocktails or excellent beers and
wines.

Gilda

: Via Mario de' Fiori 97
: Tel. 06 678 48 38

Smart club where you may
recognize a few famous faces if
you're lucky. Two restaurants and a
dance floor.

Les Griffes Café

: Via dei Prati Fiscali 401
: Tel. 06 886 433 94 or mobile
: 339 393 02 15
: Fri, Sat, discothèque from
: 11.30 p.m.

Piano bar, cabaret, live music
spread over three rooms.

Piper Club

: Via Tagliamento 9
: Tel. 06 855 53 98

Traditional disco, ever popular with
the young crowd.

Tartarughino

: Via della Scrofa 1
: Tel. 06 686 41 31

A discreet and rather suave piano
bar.

The Hard Facts

Airports
Leonardo da Vinci, or Fiumicino airport, 30 km (19 miles) south-west of the city, handles scheduled flights. It has two terminals, one for domestic and the other for international flights. Fiumicino is linked to Termini railway station (one train per hour, journey takes 30 min) and Tiburtina station (trains every 20 min; journey 40 min).

Ciampino, 15 km (9 miles) southeast of the city, is used by most charter companies.

Banks
Opening hours are Monday to Friday 8.30 a.m. until 1.20 p.m. The larger branches are also open from 2.30 to 4 p.m., but these hours may vary.

Climate
Summer, from mid-June to September, is usually very hot and stuffy. Winters are cool and often rainy. Spring and autumn are comfortably mild.

Complaints
If you have a problem in a restaurant or a shop, it's best to deal directly with the manager or the proprietor. Serious matters can be taken to the Ufficio Stranieri, Via Genova 2, tel. 06 468 629 28, open 24 hours a day.

The price of the services of a porter or a ride in a horse-drawn taxi can always be fixed in advance. If the price of a taxi-ride seems excessive, consult the tariff which is posted inside the vehicle, not forgetting all the appropriate supplements for night service, public holidays, Sundays, and so on.

Currency Exchange
At arrival points and all over the city in front of banks and post offices there are automatic exchange machines, with instructions in several languages. Exchange offices (cambio) keep the same opening hours as banks. The exchange rate varies from place to place.

Electricity
Standard current is 220V, 50 Hz AC. You will need an adaptor for continental two-pin sockets.

Emergencies
Police (carabinieri): Tel. 112
Police (municipal): Tel. 113
Fire brigade: Tel. 115
Samaritani (first aid) Tel. 118
Ambulance: Tel. 06 5510 or
   06 2430 22 22
First aid: Tel. 06 704 544 45
Help for tourists (Pronto
   intervento per turisti):
   Tel. 06 671 052 28

Duty pharmacies
Tel. 06 22 89 41
24-hour service:
Gellini
Corso Italia 100,
Tel. 06 442 497 07

Internazionale
Piazza Barberini 49
Tel. 06 482 54 56

Risorgimento
Piazza Risorgimento 44,
Tel. 06 397 381 86

Hospitals:
Ospedale G. Eastman
(dental care)
Viale Regina Elena 287B
Tel. 06 844 831

Policlinico Umberto I
Viale del Policlinico 155
Tel. 06 499 71

Entry Regulations
You will need a valid passport to enter Italy, or, if you are a citizen of an EC country, a National Identity Card. Visas are required only for stays of more than 90 days.

Events
January. A toy market is held on January 6 in the Piazza Navona to celebrate Befana.
March–April. Good Friday at the Colosseum; Via Crucis (the Way of the Cross) led by the Pope; Easter: the Easter urbi et orbi blessing in St Peter's Square. On the Trinità dei Monti steps: azaleas and street concerts.
April–May. Painting exhibitions on Via Margutta.
May. Antiques Fair on Via dei Coronari.
June. Corpus Domini at Genzano and Castelli Romani; the streets are strewn with flowers. The festival of Saint John in the Piazza di Porta San Giovanni, with porchetta, snails and fireworks.
June–July. RomaEuropa at the Villa Medici; films, dance, theatre and concerts. Expo Tevere along the Tiber; an arts and crafts market, food and wine, music and fireworks.
July. Festa de Noantri at Trastevere, processions and general rejoicing.
July–August. Arte all'aperto with opera, concerts, comedy and film at the Baths of Caracalla, at Villa Ada, Ostia Antica, by the Tiber and in the parks. Top designer fashion shows at Trinità dei Monti.
August. Festa della Madonna della Neve at Santa Maria Maggiore, where the legendary 4th-century fall of snow is recreated in a shower of flower petals.
September-October. A craft exhibition on Via dell'Orso, near Piazza Navona.
October. Wine Festival at Marino, tastings and entertainment with wine gushing from the

fountain in the main square. An Antiques exhibition in Via dei Coronari.

December. The Festa della Madonna Immacolata in Piazza di Spagna. Nativity scenes in the churches, and a life-size one in St Peter's Square. New Year's Eve is celebrated with fireworks —and watch out for plates flying from the windows.

Horse-drawn Carriages

There's nothing like a tour in a *carrozzella* for getting your bearings. You can hire one for half-an-hour or for a whole day, but agree on the price with the driver before setting out. These carriages wait at the following locations:

Piazza di Spagna, Colosseo, Fontana di Trevi, San Pietro, Via Veneto, Villa Borghese, Piazza Venezia and Piazza Navona.

Lost Property

If you have left something on the train, go to the Lost and Found Office at Termini railway station, tel. 06 473 06 682.

For property lost on a bus or the underground, tel. 06 581 60 40.

Opening Hours

Museum opening hours are extremely unreliable. In summer, the big museums open late in the evening, sometimes until 11.45 p.m. It is best to check with the tourist office, APT, who have up-to-date information.

Churches are generally open from 8.30 or 9 a.m. until noon or 1 p.m., and from 3.30 or 4 p.m. until 5 or 6.30 p.m.

Shops are usually open from Monday afternoon to Saturday 9 a.m. to 1 p.m. and 3.30 to 7.30 p.m. (in summer, from 4 to 8 p.m.). A few shops stay open non-stop from 10.30 a.m. to 7.30 p.m., even on Sunday.

In August the city is practically deserted, as it's holiday time for the Romans, including the shopkeepers.

Post Office

The Italian post office deals with mail, money transfers and telegrams. Stamps are also sold at tobacconists and often in hotels.

The Central Post Office on Piazza di San Silvestro 19 (tel. 06 679 55 30), the offices at Termini Station and Fiumicino Airport are open 24 hours per day.

In the city centre, the post offices at Via di Porta Angelica 23, Via Marmorato and Viale Mazzini 101 are open Monday to Friday 8.30 a.m.–6.30 p.m., Saturday 8.30 a.m.–1 p.m.

Public Holidays

January 1	Capodanno
January 6	Epifania (Befana)
April 25	Festa della Liberazione
May 1	Festa del Lavoro
August 15	Ferragosto

November 1	Ognissanti
December 8	Immacolata Concezione
December 25	Natale
December 26	Santo Stefano
Moveable	Lunedì di Pasqua

For special events, see pp. 59–60.

Public Transport

Rome is served by the orange buses, a few trams and an electric mini-bus, No. 119, which covers the historic centre.

For a tour of the city, take bus no. 110 from Termini Station, Piazza dei Cinquecento, daily from April 1 to September 30, every 30 minutes, 9 a.m.–8 p.m. October 1 to March 31, 10 a.m.–6 p.m. For reservations call 06 4695 22 22. A ticket costs €7.74.

Most main bus terminals are in the city centre: Piazza dei Cinquecento, Piazza Venezia, Largo Augusto Imperatore, Piazzale Flaminio, Piazza Risorgimento, Piazzale Clodio and Piazza Mancini (near the Olympic Stadium).

Ask for a free bus map at the offices of the ATAC, Piazza del Risorgimento and Piazza dei Cinquecento.

The Rome underground, run by COTRAL, has only two lines: **A** (red) Vatican–Tuscolana **B** (blue) Rebibbia–EUR.

Certain stops are close to major monuments: the Vatican, Piazza del Popolo, Piazza Spagna, Piazza Barberini, Termini Station, Colosseum, Circo Massimo. Trains run every 8 minutes from 5.30 a.m. to 11.30 p.m., and every 30 minutes during the night.

Tickets

On sale in the underground stations, at the bus terminals, in bars and at tobacconists and newspaper kiosks. Tickets for surface transport are valid for 75 minutes and cost €0.77: you can change lines with the same ticket. Underground tickets are valid for only one journey. A book of 11 tickets costs €7.70, a BIG ticket is valid for a whole day and costs €3.10. A weekly card (CIS) is available for €12.40.

To validate the ticket, enter the bus at the back and punch the ticket in the machine. If you have a day or week ticket, you can enter at the front.

Religious Services

Mass is celebrated in Italian in all Catholic churches.
Other denominations:
Church of England
Ognissanti,
via del Babuino 153B
tel. 06 3600 18 81
Comunitá Ebraica (Synagogue)
Lungotevere Cenci
tel. 06 684 00 61
Chiesa Evangelica Metodista (Methodist)
Via Firenze 38
tel. 06 81 48 11

**Centro Islamico-Moschea
di Roma** (Mosque)
Viale della Moschea,
tel. 06 808 22 58

Church of Scotland
(Presbyterian)
Sant'Andrea
Via XX Settembre 7
tel. 06 482 76 27

Taxis

Cabs are yellow with an illuminated "Taxi" sign on the roof; they line up at ranks and are not obliged to stop if you hail one in the street. Avoid the pirate taxis which lurk around the monuments and stations. For a Radio Taxi, call 06 88 22, 06 49 94 or 06 35 70. The tariff depends on the distance, with various supplements charged for the initial hiring fee, luggage, night service, etc. Taxi drivers expect a 10 per cent tip.

Telephone

The telephone boxes which are scattered throughout the city require phone cards, which can be purchased from post offices, bars, tobacconists, some newspaper kiosks, the headquarters of Italian telecommunications and railway stations. Calls can also be made from a public telephone centre where you pay at the counter once you have finished speaking. There are several in the city, at Termini railway station, at the airport, in the underground car park at the Villa Borghese, and at the Palazzo delle Poste, Piazza San Silvestro, open 24 hours a day. For directory inquiries, dial 12.

The outgoing international code is 00. Then dial the country code (UK 44; USA and Canada 1) and the area code without the initial zero, followed by the local number.

Tipping

Service is included in the bill in restaurants, but you can always leave a few extra coins. It is normal to tip your hotel porter and anyone who carries out a personal service.

Tourist Office

City maps and brochures are available from the offices of the APT (Azienda Provinciale per il Turismo):
Via Parigi 11, tel. 06 488 99 253
Centro Visitatori, Via Parigi 5 (Piazza della Repubblica), Monday to Saturday 9 a.m.–7 p.m.
Stazione Termini
tel. 06 874 064 80
Fiumicino, tel. 06 659 544 71
ENIT (Italian Tourist Office): Via Marghera 2–6, tel. 06 497 11.
The green kiosks all over town, Punti Informativi Turistici (PIT), are run by the municipality and provide information in several languages.
Call Center: 06 360 043 99
www.romaturismo.com

GENERAL EDITOR
Barbara Ender-Jones
RESEARCH
Francesca Grazzi
and Farid Rahimi
PHOTO CREDITS
Renata Holzbachová:
pp. 5, 41;
Hémisphères/Lescourret: p. 1;
Hémisphères/Wysocki: pp. 2,
23, inside front cover;
Hémisphères/Frances:
pp. 9, 16, 30, 33, 37, 46
MAPS
Elsner & Schichor;
JPM Publications

Copyright © 2003, 1997
by JPM Publications S.A.
12, avenue William-Fraisse,
1006 Lausanne, Switzerland
E-mail:
information@jpmguides.com
Web site:
http://www.jpmguides.com/

Printed in Switzerland
Weber/Bienne (CTP) — 03/07/01
Edition 2003–2004

The Italian Way

Greetings

The Italians appreciate your greeting them with a *"buon giorno"* (literally "good day") or *"buona sera"* ("good evening"). Save *"buona notte"* ("good night") for when you're off to bed. Add *"come sta?"* ("how are you?") and your Italian had better be good enough to understand the answer. With luck, your accent will give you away and people will be kind enough just to answer *"bene, grazie"* ("well, thank you") and not give you a rundown on their ailments and tax problems. If they are the first to ask, reply: *"Bene, grazie"* and add: *"E lei?"* ("And you?"). The proper response to *"grazie"* by itself is *"prego"* ("don't mention it"). Make your way through a crowded bus with a polite *"Permesso"* ("May I?").

Men and women shake hands on a first meeting. With a woman, once you've struck up a friendship, exchange a light kiss on each cheek, usually an airy affair to avoid lipstick marks or misunderstandings. Down south, men commonly exchange a Godfatherly bearhug. It's quite harmless.

DON'T BE SHY

To help you with your spoken Italian we provide a very simple transcription alongside the phrases. You may not end up sounding like a native speaker but people will be pleased to hear you trying. Syllables in capital letters should be stressed.

Good morning/ afternoon.	Buon giorno.	bwohn JOHR-noh
Good evening.	Buona sera.	BWOH-nah SEH-rah
Goodbye.	Arrivederci.	ahr-ree-veh-DEHR-chee
See you later.	A più tardi.	ah pyoo TAHR-dee
Hi!/Bye!	Ciao!	CHAA-oh
Yes/No.	Sì/No.	see/noh
Maybe.	Forse.	FOHR-seh
That's fine/Okay.	D'accordo.	dah-KOHR-doh
That's right!	Va bene.	vah BEH-neh
Please.	Per favore.	pehr fah-VAW-reh
Thank you/Thanks.	Grazie.	GRAA-tsyeh
Thank you very much.	Tante grazie.	TAHN-teh GRAA-tsyeh
You're welcome.	Prego.	PREH-goh
Nice to meet you.	Molto lieto.	MOHL-toh LYEH-toh
How are you?	Come sta?	KAW-meh stah
Well, thanks.	Bene, grazie.	BEH-neh, GRAA-tsyeh
And you?	E lei?	eh lay
Pardon me.	Mi scusi.	mee SKOO-zee
I'm sorry.	Mi dispiace.	mee dee-SPYAA-cheh
Don't mention it.	Non c'è di che.	nohn cheh dee keh
Excuse me...	Scusi...	SKOO-zee
My name is...	Mi chiamo...	mee KYAA-moh
I don't understand.	Non capisco.	nohn kah-PEE-skoh
Slowly, please.	Parli piano.	PAHR-lee PYAA-noh
Could you say that again?	Può ripetere, per favore?	pwoh ree-PEH-teh-reh, pehr fah-VAW-reh
Do you speak English?	Parla inglese?	PAHR-lah eeng-GLEH-zeh
I don't speak much Italian.	Non parlo bene l'italiano.	nohn PAHR-loh BEH-neh lee-tah-LYAA-noh
Please write it down.	Per favore, me lo scriva.	pehr fah-VAW-reh, meh loh SKREE-vah
I understand.	Capisco.	kah-PEE-skoh
Let's go.	Andiamo.	ahn-DYAA-moh

Getting around

Official metered yellow taxis line up at railway stations or outside the major hotels, only rarely hailed when they are on the move. Beware of pirate drivers, identifiable by the fact that *they* approach you. Unauthorized cars are called in Italian *abusivi,* which says it all. Expect legitimate extras on the meter price, charged particularly on night trips, on several pieces of luggage or on rides to or from the airport—rates are posted in the vehicle. Add a 10 per cent tip.

Public transport. Services for the bus *(autobus)* vary— they are good in Florence and Milan, overcrowded in Rome and Naples. The water-bus in Venice *(vaporetto* or smaller, faster *motoscafo)* is best of all—like a cheerful cruise along the canals through centuries of history. The number of the bus lines and the route served are displayed at each bus stop *(fermata)*. For cheaper fares, buy a book of tickets *(blocchetto di biglietti)* at news-stands or tobacconists. Get on through the door marked *"Salita"* and off at the exit marked *"Uscita"*. Subway trains, *Metro(politano),* operate in Milan and Rome; the tickets are interchangeable with the bus system.

Trains. Besides the luxury international *EuroCity* (EC) and the *Intercity* (IC), there's the *Rapido,* faster than the crowded *Espresso.* The *Diretto* is slower and the *Locale* slower still, stopping at every halt, seemingly for anyone who cares to whistle it down.

Taxi, please!	Taxi!	TAH-ksee
Are you free?	È libero?	eh LEE-beh-roh
Hotel Paradiso, please.	Hotel Paradiso, per favore.	oh-TEHL pah-rah-DEE-zoh, pehr fah-VAW-reh
To the airport/ the station, please.	All'aeroporto/ alla stazione, per favore.	ahl-lah-eh-roh-POHR-toh/ AHL-lah stah-TSYAW-neh, pehr fah-VAW-reh
I'm in a hurry.	Ho fretta.	oh FREHT-tah
Please stop here.	Si fermi qui.	see FEHR-mee kwee
Please wait for me.	Aspetti un momento, per favore.	ah-SPEHT-tee oon moh-MEHN-toh, pehr fah-VAW-reh
How much is it?	Quant'è?	kwahn-TEH
Keep the change.	Tenga il resto.	TEHNG-gah eel REH-stoh
Where is the bus stop?	Dov'è la fermata dell'autobus?	daw-VEH la fer-MAH-tah dehl-LA-oo-toh-boos
When does the next bus leave?	Quando parte il prossimo bus?	KWAHN-doh PAR-teh eel PROHS-see-moh boos
Where is the metro, please?	Dov'è il metrò, per favore?	daw-VEH eel meh-TROH, pehr fah-VAW-reh
A book of tickets, please.	Un blocchetto di biglietti, per favore.	oon blohk-KEHT-toh dee bee-LYEHT-tee, pehr fah-VAW-reh
one-way	andata	ahn-DAA-tah
round-trip	andata e ritorno	ahn-DAA-tah eh ree-TOHR-noh
first class	prima classe	PREE-mah KLAHS-seh
second class	seconda classe	seh-KOHN-dah KLAHS-seh
platform	binario	bee-NAA-ryoh
toilets	gabinetti	gah-bee-NEHT-tee
Is this seat free?	È libero questo posto?	eh LEE-beh-roh KWEH-stoh POH-stoh
strike	sciopero	SHOH-peh-roh

Accommodation

Your hotel lobby is where you first learn how much Italians like their titles. You'll get better service if you call the hall-porter or bell-captain *portiere,* as opposed to *facchino* (baggage porter or bellhop). Upstairs, the room maid is *cameriera.* Hotel tipping also has its fine distinctions: on the spot to porters for carrying bags or other incidental services, but a lump sum to room maids at the end of the stay.

Ratings for the hotel *(hotel* or *albergo)* range from luxury five-star to rudimentary one-star. Expect in-house laundry and dry-cleaning services only from three-star and better. Breakfast is generally optional (and not particularly copious) but in high season, resort hotels often insist on at least half-board. A separate rating system is used for boarding houses *(pensione),* ranging from very comfortable, with excellent family cooking, to modest, providing just the basic services. Humble accommodation in monasteries run by monks is very different from the often luxurious amenities of converted monasteries run by hoteliers.

If you have checked out of your hotel, you can still take a *siesta* and bath in a low-price day hotel *(albergo diurno),* usually close to the main railway station.

I've a reservation	Ho fatto una prenotazione	oh FAHT-toh oo-nah preh-noh-ta-TSYAW-neh
Here's the confirmation/voucher.	Ecco la conferma/il buono.	EHK-koh lah kohn-FEHR-mah/ eel BWAW-noh
a single room	una camera singola	OO-nah KAA-meh-rah SEENG-goh-lah
a double	una camera doppia	OO-nah KAA-meh-rah DOHP-pyah
twin beds	letti gemelli	LEHT-tee jeh-MEHL-lee
double bed	letto matrimoniale	LEHT-toh mah-tree-moh-NYAA-leh
with a bath/shower	con bagno/doccia	kohn BAH-nyoh/ DOHT-chah
Can I see the room?	Posso vedere la camera?	POHS-so veh-DEH-reh lah KAH-meh-rah
My key, please.	La mia chiave, per favore.	lah MEE-ah KYAA-veh, pehr fah-VAW-reh
Is there mail for me?	C'è posta per me?	cheh POH-stah pehr meh
I need:	Ho bisogno di:	oh bee-ZAW-nyoh dee
hangers	grucce	GROOT-che
soap	una saponetta	OO-nah sah-poh-NEHT-tah
a blanket	una coperta	OO-nah koh-PEHR-tah
an (extra) pillow	un guanciale (in più)	oon gwahn-CHAA-leh (een pyoo)
This is for the laundry.	Questo è da lavare.	KWEH-stoh eh dah lah-VAA-reh
These are clothes to be cleaned/ pressed.	Questi sono vestiti da pulire/ stirare.	KWEH-stee SAW-noh veh-STEE-tee dah poo-LEE-reh/stee-RAA-reh
Urgently.	È urgente.	eh oor-JEHN-teh
I'm checking out.	Lascio l'albergo.	LAHSH-shoh lahl-BEHR-goh
I'd like to pay	Vorrei pagare	vohr-RAY pah-GAA-reh
by credit card	con carta di credito.	kohn KAHR-tah dee KREH-dee-toh

Buon appetito!

The advantage of the ordinary *trattoria* restaurant over the more formal (and higher priced) establishment known as a *ristorante* is usually apparent as soon as you walk in. Much of the day's "menu" is appetizingly laid out on a long table or refrigerated counter. The display includes not only cold starters *(antipasti)* but also fish *(pesce)* or other seafood *(frutti di mare)* and even cuts of meat *(carne)*. State your cooking preference: *alla griglia* (grilled), *fritto* (fried) or *al forno* (baked). The *pasta* of course is in the kitchen, but these days it comes in literally hundreds of different shapes and sizes—manufacturers even have architects to design new forms to enhance the different sauces.

At midday, you may prefer the stand-up bar known as *tavola calda,* where you can get sandwiches and a hot or cold dish at the counter. Better than fast-food is the *panino ripieno,* a bread roll stuffed with cold meats, sausage, salad or cheese—your personal choice from the counter-display—the original of the American "submarine".

YOU AND YOU

There are several ways of saying "you" in Italian. *Tu* (plural *voi*) is familiar, used for children, friends, family. *Lei* (plural *loro*) is polite, for people you don't know well. And if you meet the person of your dreams, "I love you" is *Ti amo*.

English	Italian	Pronunciation
I'm hungry/thirsty.	Ho fame/sete.	oh FAA-meh/SEH-teh
A table for two, please.	Un tavolo per due, per favore.	oon TAA-voh-loh pehr DOO-eh, pehr fa-VAW-reh
The menu	Il menù	eel meh-NOO
The fixed menu	Il menú fisso	eel meh-NOO FEES-soh
I'm a vegetarian.	Sono vegetariano(a).	SAW-noh veh-jeh-tah-RYAA-noh(ah)
A glass of water.	Un bicchiere d'acqua.	oon-beek-KYEH-reh DAHK-kwah
I'd like a beer.	Vorrei una birra.	vohr-RAY oo-nah BEER-rah.
The wine list.	La carte dei vini.	lah KAHR-tah day VEE-nee
A bottle of red/ white/rosé wine.	Una bottiglia di vino rosso/ bianco/rosato.	oo-nah boht-TEE-lyah dee VEE-noh ROHS-soh/ BYANG-koh/roh-ZAA-toh
beef	manzo	MAHN-dzoh
bread	pane	PAA-neh
butter	burro	BOOR-roh
cheese	formaggio	fohr-MAHD-joh
chicken	pollo	POHL-loh
coffee	caffè	kahf-FEH
fish	pesce	PEHSH-sheh
fruit juice	succo di frutta	SOOK-koh dee FROOT-tah
ice cream	gelato	jeh-LAA-toh
meat	carne	KAHR-neh
milk	latte	LAHT-teh
mineral water	acqua minerale	AHK-kwah mee-neh-RAA-leh
fizzy/flat	gasata/naturale	gah-ZAA-tah/ nah-too-RAA-leh
mustard	senape	SEH-nah-peh
pork	maiale	mah-YAA-leh
salt and pepper	sale e pepe	SAA-leh eh PEH-peh
tea	tè	teh
vegetables	verdura	vehr-DOO-rah
The bill	Il conto	eel KOHN-toh

Telephone

You'll soon notice that on the telephone, the Italians do not reply with *Buon giorno* but *"Pronto!"* It means literally that the caller is "ready" to speak, a national characteristic. If you are answering the phone, in all likelihood, your next phrase should be *"Parla inglese?"* ("Do you speak English?") If the answer is *"No"*, try *"Qui parla..."* ("This is ... speaking").

Italy now has a modern, privatized telephone network, and just about everybody walks around talking into a mobile phone. Public telephones *(cabina telefonica)* function with phone cards, which can be purchased at post offices, some newspaper kiosks, the headquarters of Italian telecommunications and railway stations. They do not work until you tear off the corner. There are also Internet Cafés in every town, so you can keep in touch with your e-mails.

To call the US and Canada direct, dial 001. For the UK, the country code is 0044. Note that for local calls, you have to dial the whole number, including the initial 0.

May I use this phone?	Posso usare questo telefono?	POHS-soh oo-ZAA-reh KWEH-stoh teh-LEH-foh-noh
Can I reverse the charges?	Posso telefonare a carico del destinatario?	POHS-soh teh-leh-foh-NAA-reh ah KAA-ree-koh dehl deh-stee-nah-TOH-ryoh

---

HAPPY TALK

Enrich your vocabulary and sprinkle your conversation with a few useful, cheery adjectives: *simpatico* (charming), *splendido* (magnificent), *fantastico* (terrific), *formidabile* (tremendous), *divertente* (amusing), *piacevole* (pleasant), *allegro* (happy).

Wrong number.	Numero sbagliato.	NOO-meh-roh zbah-LYAA-toh
Speak more slowly.	Parli più piano.	PAHR-lee pyoo PYAA-noh
Could you take a message?	Può prendere un messaggio?	pwoh PREHN-deh-reh oon mehs-SAHD-joh
My number is…	Il mio numero è il…	eel MEE-oh NOO-meh-roh eh eel
My room number is…	Il mio numero di camera è il…	eel MEE-oh NOO-meh-roh dee KAA-meh-rah eh eel
Do you sell stamps?	Avete dei francobolli?	ah-VEH-teh day frahng-koh-BOHL-lee
How much is it to Great Britain/ the United States?	Quanto è per la Gran Bretagna/ gli Stati Uniti?	KWAHN-toh eh pehr lah grahn breh-TAH-nyah/ lyee STAA-tee oo-NEE-tee
I'd like to mail this parcel.	Vorrei spedire questo pacco.	vohr-RAY speh-DEE-reh KWEH-sto PAHK-koh
Can I send a fax?	Posso mandare un fax?	POHS-soh mahn-DAA-reh oon fahks
Can I make a photocopy here?	Posso fare una fotocopia qui?	POHS-soh FAA-reh OO-nah foh-toh-KAW-pyah kwee
Where's the mailbox?	Dov'è la cassetta delle lettere?	daw-VEH lah kahs-SEHT-tah DEHL-leh LEHT-teh-reh
registered letter	lettera raccomandata	LEHT-teh-rah rahk-kohm-mahn-DAA-tah
air mail	via aerea	VEE-ah ah-EH-reh-ah
postcard	cartolina postale	kahr-toh-LEE-nah poh-STAA-leh

NUMBERS			
1 uno	6 sei	11 undici	16 sedici
2 due	7 sette	12 dodici	17 diciassette
3 tre	8 otto	13 tredici	18 diciotto
4 quattro	9 nove	14 quattordici	19 diciannove
5 cinque	10 dieci	15 quindici	20 venti

Money matters

Italy has adopted the Euro, and it makes life simple (it's just like using dollars). Coins are issued in denominations of 1, 2, 5, 10, 20 and 50 euro cents *(centesimi)*, 1 and 2 euros. Banknotes: 5, 10, 20, 50, 100, 200 and 500 euros.

The better exchange rate you get at the bank compared with the hotel is offset by the amount of time spent waiting in line, often one to make the initial transaction and another to collect the cash. Have your passport with you. In most places, banks are open Monday to Friday, 8.30 a.m. to 1.30 p.m. and another hour in mid-afternoon. Railway station and airport currency exchange offices stay open longer, and weekends as well. Most convenient of all – as long as you know your PIN – are the automatic cash dispensers for international credit cards (at stations and main tourist centres), but you will have to pay a commission.

QUESTION MARK

To ask a question in Italian, all you have to do is change the inflexion of your voice, lifting it towards the end of the sentence:

It's far away.	**È lontano.**
It's far?	**È lontano?**

bank	banca	BAHN-kah
currency exchange	cambio	KAHM-byoh
Where can I change money?	Dove posso cambiare del denaro?	DAW-veh POHS-soh kahm-BYAA-reh dehl deh-NAA-roh
Can you cash a travellers cheque?	Può incassare un travellers cheque?	pwoh een-kahs-SAA-reh oon "travellers check"
I want to change dollars/pounds.	Voglio cambiare dei dollari/ delle sterline.	VOH-lyoh kahm-BYAA-reh day DOHL-lah-ree/ DEHL-leh stehr-LEE-neh
Will this credit card do?	Accetta questa carta di credito?	aht-CHEHT-tah KWEH-stah KAHR-tah dee KREH-dee-toh
Can you help me? Just looking…	Può aiutarmi? Sto solo guardando…	pwoh ah-yoo-TAAR-mee stoh SAW-loh gwahr-DAHN-doh
How much is this?	Quant'è?	kwahn-TEH
cheap	buon mercato	bwohn mehr-KAA-toh
expensive	caro	KAA-roh
Can I try it on?	Posso provarlo?	POHS-soh proh-VAHR-loh
I don't know the European sizes.	Non conosco le taglie europee.	nohn koh-NOH-skoh leh TAA-lyeh eh-oo-roh-PEH-eh
It's too big/small	È troppo grande/ piccolo.	eh trop-poh GRAN-deh/ PEE-koh-loh
I'll think about it.	Voglio pensarci.	VOH-lyoh pehn-SAHR-chee
I'll buy it.	Lo prendo.	loh PREHN-doh
A receipt, please.	Una ricevuta, per favore.	OO-nah ree-cheh-VOO-tah, pehr fah-VAW-reh
antique shop	antiquario	ahn-tee-KWAA-ryoh
bakery	panetteria	pah-neht-teh-REE-ah
bookshop	libreria	lib-reh-REE-ah
pharmacy	farmacia	fahr-mah-CHEE-ah
jewellery store	gioielleria	joh-yehl-leh-REE-ah
pastry shop	pasticceria	pah-steet-cheh-REE-ah
shoe shop	calzoleria	kal-tsoh-leh-REE-ah
supermarket	supermercato	soo-pehr-mehr-KAA-toh

Health and Safety

The best planned vacation may sometimes be spoiled—by a stomach upset or something of the sort. Too much sun, too much Chianti in the middle of the day and you'll be looking around for the chemists *(farmacia)*. One of them is open somewhere in town, even nights and weekends. Most often, it's located near the main railway station.

If you're prone to something that needs special medication, take a supply from home since, as good as most Italian medicine is, you may not be able to find precisely the same prescription on the spot. The emergency number to dial for first aid is **118**, and for an ambulance **113**.

Safety First. There's no need to be paranoid, but it's silly to take pointless risks. The precautions are simple, and the same as in big towns anywhere in the world. Leave your valuables in the hotel's safe *(cassaforte)* and carry only as much cash as you need. Keep your passport separate from your travellers cheques and credit cards. If you have rented a car, don't park it with bags visible on the seats. Always be on the alert for pickpockets in crowded places.

Police come in two kinds: *Vigili Urbani* (municipal police) in navy blue uniforms or all white in summer; and *Carabinieri* in brown or black, handling major crimes and street-demonstrations.

Emergency number for the police: **112**

I don't feel well.	Non mi sento bene.	nohn mee SEHN-toh BEH-neh
Where is a chemists?	Dov'è una farmacia?	daw-VEH OO-nah fahr-mah-CHEE-ah
an upset stomach	un'indigestione	oon-een-dee-jeh-STYAW-neh
an injury	una ferita	OO-nah feh-REE-tah
toothache	mal di denti	mahl dee DEHN-tee
headache	mal di testa	mahl dee TEH-stah
I feel pain…	Mi fa male…	mee fah MAA-leh
… in my leg	… la gamba	lah GAHM-bah
… in my arm	… il braccio	eel BRAH-choh
… in my stomach	… lo stomaco	loh STOM-mah-koh
… in my chest	… il petto	eel PEHT-toh
I am bleeding.	Perdo sangue.	PEHR-doh SANG-gweh
I need a doctor.	Ho bisogno di un dottore.	oh bee-ZAW-nyoh dee oon doht-TAW-reh
Can you give me a prescription?	Può darmi una ricetta?	pwoh DAHR-mee OO-nah ree-CHEHT-tah
Help!	Aiuto!	ah-YOO-toh
Stop thief!	Al ladro!	ahl LAA-droh
Leave me alone.	Mi lasci in pace.	mee LASH-shee een PAA-cheh
I've lost my wallet/ passport.	Ho perso il portafogli/ il passaporto.	oh PEHR-soh eel pohr-tah FAW-lyee/ eel pahs-sah-POHR-toh
My credit cards have been stolen.	Mi hanno rubato le carte di credito.	mee AHN-noh roo-BAA-toh leh KAHR-teh dee KREH-dee-toh
I'm lost.	Mi sono perso.	mee SAW-noh PEHR-soh
Where's the police station/the hospital?	Dov'è la polizia/ l'ospedale?	daw-VEH lah poh-lee TSEE-ah/ loh-speh-DAA-leh
I have been assaulted.	Sono stato aggredito.	SAW-noh STAA-to ahg-greh-DEE-toh
witness	testimone	tes-tee-MOH-neh
lawyer	avvocato	av-voh-KAH-toh

Illustrations: Sofie Czaplejewicz

EVERY LETTER COUNTS

In Italian, every letter of the word is pronounced distinctly, so when a letter is doubled you have to pronounce it twice: *frutto* is "frut to", *delle* "del le", *birra* "bir ra", and so on.

NOTICES

The meaning of some signs you'll see:

Chiuso	Closed	*Signore (Donne)*	Ladies
Entrata (Ingresso)	Entrance	*Signori (Uomini)*	Gentlemen
Guasto	Out of order	*Uscita*	Exit
Occupato	Occupé	*Vietato*	Forbidden

FALSE FRIENDS

Many Italian words look like direct equivalents of English words, but you could be very wrong:

camera	room	*magazzino*	warehouse
conveniente	cheap, inexpensive	*moneta*	coins, change
fresco	cool	*morbido*	soft
incidente	accident	*pila*	battery (transistor)
libreria	bookstore	*slip*	underpants

JPM Publications • *Specialists in customized guides*

Neither the publisher nor his client can be held responsible in any way for omissions or errors.
Av. William-Fraisse 12, 1006 Lausanne, Suisse
Copyright© 2003, 1999 JPM Publications SA
www.jpmguides.com/ Printed in Switzerland – 0/304 – (CTP)

**AROUND
THE QUIRINALE**

300 m

300 yd

N

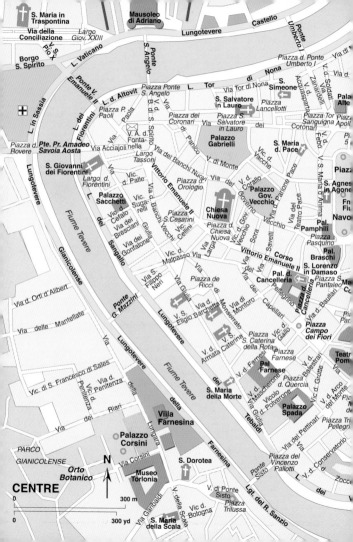

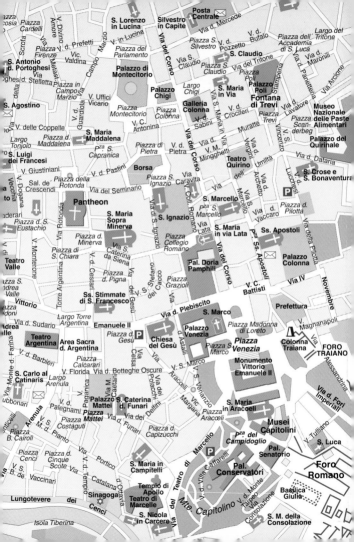